Leadership in Government

The Art of Work

100 Ways for Working
Effectively in Government

Leadership in Government

The Art of Work

| 100 Ways for Working Effectively in Government |

MADAN MOHAN UPADHYAY, I.A.S.

Manjul Publishing House

First published in India by

Manjul Publishing House
• C-16, Sector 3, Noida, Uttar Pradesh 201301, India
Website: www.manjulindia.com

Registered Office:
• 10, Nishat Colony, Bhopal 462 003 – India

Copyright © Madan Mohan Upadhyay 2011
All rights reserved

This edition first published in 2011 by Pentagon Press

This revised edition first published by
Manjul Publishing House Pvt. Ltd. in 2022

ISBN 978-93-5543-125-7

Printed and bound in India by Repro India Ltd.

The content of the book is the sole expression and opinion of its authors, and not necessarily that of the publisher. No warranties or guarantees are expressed or implied by the publisher's choice to include any of the content in this volume. The publisher shall not be liable for any physical, psychological, emotional, financial, or commercial damages, including but not limited to, special, incidental, consequential or other damages.

All rights reserved. No part of this book may be used or reproduced, stored in or introduced into a retrieval system, or transmitted, in any form, or by any means (electronic, mechanical, photocopying, recording or otherwise) without the prior written permission of the copyright owners. Any person who does any unauthorized act in relation to this publication may be liable to criminal prosecution and civil claims for damages.

To my parents

Contents

Acknowledgements   *xi*
Introduction   *xiii*

1. Take the Lead   1
2. Seeing is Believing   5
3. Keep Pace   7
4. Management and Leadership   10
5. What is My Current Role?   13
6. Just Do It   16
7. Monitor, Monitor and Monitor   21
8. Keep Continuous Trajectory Controls   25
9. Consolidate the Gains   27
10. Pilot Locally – Expand Regionally   30
11. Communicate – Baat Nikalegi to Phir Dur Talak Jayegi   33
12. Blow Your Own Trumpet   39
13. There is Only One Life – Your Job Can Give Purpose to It   42
14. A Visual Reminder – the Focus   46
15. People Quotient   48
16. Integrity – Something Beyond Compromise   50
17. Good or Bad – Decide Either Way   54
18. There is Plenty of Room at the Top   57
19. Bureaucratic Organisations – Positional Leadership   59

20.	It's All About Political Goals	62
21.	Innovation All the Way	65
22.	The Buck Stops Here – Provide Solution to the Organisational Problems	70
23.	Leaders – We All Need Them	74
24.	Leadership for All	77
25.	Anticipation and Action	79
26.	Quality – Let Our Work Speak About It	81
27.	Working in Style – the Branding	85
28.	See the Big Picture and Share it	87
29.	Time Matters	89
30.	The Well Prepared Leader	93
31.	Take Responsibility for Action	94
32.	Change the Rules – Know the Rules	96
33.	Bench Mark – Set the Work Standards	99
34.	Identify Key Strategic Intervention	101
35.	Change – Do it Quickly	104
36.	Guide Them	108
37.	Love Your Self: Love Your Work	110
38.	Self Belief	112
39.	The More We Do – The More We Can Do	115
40.	Consolidate and Publish	117
41.	Know Your Organisation	120
42.	Vision	122
43.	Own the Organization	126
44.	Let the Office Speak – Give a Facelift	129
45.	Make Your Team	131
46.	Look Out for Ideas	134
47.	Passion that Transcends the 10 to 5 Mindset	137
48.	The Critical Mass for a Tornado	140
49.	Work – the Play Called Government	142

50.	The Upward Helix: It's a Continuous Growth Route	145
51.	Governments are Unique	148
52.	Governance and Government	151
53.	Use of I.T. – Government @ the Speed of Light	154
54.	Growth Continuum-Growing Up With the Organisation	158
55.	Keep the Team Motivated	160
56.	Competence – Let it Grow All Around	162
57.	Take Responsibility for Action	165
58.	Bureaucratic Accountability	168
59.	Declutter the Work Place	170
60.	Work Called Play	172
61.	Tatkal Sewa	175
62.	Meetings and Minutes	176
63.	Jump the Levels	178
64.	Seeing is Believing and Eye Opening Too	181
65.	Daily Continuous Learning	185
66.	Stay Ahead	186
67.	Work Hard – Party Hard	187
68.	Fun at Workplace	188
69.	Prevent the Cost Over Run	190
70.	Dress for Success	192
71.	Give Result Not Excuses	194
72.	Unwanted Papers – Destroy them Immediately	196
73.	Change – the Only Certainty At All Level	198
74.	Love Your Self: Love Your Work	201
75.	Small Steps – Keep Moving	204
76.	Continuous Search for Excellence Through Innovation	207
77.	Creativity for Every One	210
78.	Empower the Team	213

79.	Give New Armaments	217
80.	Awards & Rewards	221
81.	Perform	227
82.	Motivated Work Force – The Charge That Generates the Force	232
83.	Getting Out of the Comfort Zone	236
84.	Evaluate	239
85.	Tapping the Untapped Potential –Releasing the Power of Hanuman	242
86.	The Team that Works – Selecting the Right Person	247
87.	Our Everyday Heros	250
88.	Let Each Individual Be Accountable	252
89.	Stay Fit	256
90.	Efficiency at Work	260
91.	Capacity Building	262
92.	Keep the Team Motivated	265
93.	Competence – Let it Grow All Around	267
94.	Manage Your Personal Matters	271
95.	Clean Up – Speed Up & Save	274
96.	Citizen Focused Agenda	275
97.	Media – The Friend, Philosopher, Critic and Guide	277
98.	Reorganise to Optimise	281
99.	Show What You Talk – The Photographer Friend	285
100.	The Well Prepared Leader	288

LEADERSHIP IN GOVERNMENT

The Art of Work

100 Ways for Working Effectively in Government

All leaders are agents of change. If they are not, they cannot be called leaders. It is a positive, conscious change from being led to being the leader – a transformation that is the precursor to success.

Government is the single largest driving force in civil society, and synergic, harmonious action by leaders in government can rapidly lead us to our goals. It must be realised that merely an industrial growth of 8 to 9 percent does not give the complete picture. The power of the silent, sleeping giant called public organization remains to be harnessed.

-From the Introduction

Leadership in Government - The Art of Work is about performance and results, not about management principles or models. It talks about how the workforce in various government Organisations across the country can make itself more productive by understanding and practicing small steps that will result in making them better people as well as better civil servants. This is an incisive book about 100 important aspects of working effectively in government. It will make those who head government organizations at various levels reassess their roles and realign themselves with a vision that is inclusive and driven by passion, to spread efficiency and, as a result, satisfaction, through effective and result oriented performance.

Acknowledgements

I love innovative approaches which have always helped me in achieving better results. The past thirty years in public services across different organization in Central and State governments in various capacities has given me an opportunity to see organizational behavior from an insider's perspective. The positive organizational changes which various initiatives had brought out inspired me to share them with other colleagues at various forums. During lectures at the Indian Institute of Management Indore and Academy of Public Administration, Bhopal, my concepts on public services were further refined and I thought I should pen them in a book.

My association with the Institute of Good Governance & Policy Analysis, Bhopal too has helped me in experimenting with these ideas.

I thank all my former and present colleagues & friends who have in the past years have helped me in better understanding of the real work place problems and helped in finding solutions. It is not possible to name all of them but I owe my gratitude to them for shaping these ideas that constitute the Art of Work.

17 May 2022   **Madan Mohan Upadhyay, I.A.S.**

Introduction

This book has been written for all levels in government. We keep hearing about the crisis of leadership, failure of system, non responsiveness etc. Most of it boils down to, who is leading the organization? It can be a small office of a dozen employees or an organization of more than a million like the Indian Army and the Railways.

Today our country is at a stage where we are aiming to be world leaders and hope to surpass all major global economies including US and China. Growth of a country is not necessarily judged by the economic indicators like GDP or the % annual growth, there are innumerable other aspects on which the nation has to act in harmony and thereby generate a crescendo effect that results in quantum growth – A growth that is significant and sustainable. This needs leadership at every level in government and in its public sector undertaking, in fact the complete spectrum of executive and technical manpower that constitute the workforce called government.

Leadership is a subject which is probably most extensively written and talked about, yet it remains a mystery for many. Leadership is no longer a charisma or something which one inherits. We all have been doing it in smaller ways in our daily life. This book has tried to give it a specific focus-**leadership in government**. I have noticed that immense literature and case studies are available on the corporate sector but very little is available about governmental organisations. This book has specifically addressed that sector, a sector which is entrusted with the responsibility of providing wheels to the rapid pace of development. Leadership is not something which you just discover by chance, it is something that is taught, learned and developed and the more once practices, the better it becomes. The book dwells upon the various key aspects of leadership in government and the art called work.

The book has identified key inputs which can be applied to all organisations in government. These are based on certain principles and ideas which have been successfully implemented in our own country and have resulted in phenomenal transformation. The various chapters and the ideas contained in them can be implemented by every one and see the positive changes in a short period. The book takes you out of the manager mode (managing whatever have been given to you or doing things right) to the leadership mode (taking the organisation to newer heights or doing the right things) via systematic intervention and innovation.

Government is the single largest driving force and the synergetic actions by its leaders can rapidly take us to our goal. It be realised that mere industrial growth of 8 to 9% through the organised or the unorganised industrial sector is not the complete story. The power of the silent giant called the public organisations remains to be harnessed. Million of these employees and thousands of organisational leaders can put the nation on fast track and then sustain it.

The book has put in place the keys to success in government. The strategies can as well be used in other organisations as they too broadly follow some common management principles.

It would be of interest to government watchers outside the government too.

Bhopal   **Madan Mohan Upadhyay**
17 January 2010

1

Take the Lead

"Inventories can be managed, but people must be led."
                                                    H. Ross Perot

The word leadership is made of two words, Leader and Ship. It is like leading a ship. Leading, means you have to be in front and like the captain of the ship take responsibility for

1. Everything a ship (the organization) represents
2. Its directions – the destination
3. Its speed
4. The mid course management.

This has been well captured in a couplet

Hamare ghar to hain paani pe tairne wale
Hawa ke rukh ko samajhana bahut jaruri hai

Meaning, that we have homes floating on water, and it is essential to know which direction the wind is blowing.

Those of us who have rowed a boat in flowing river know that it is more than just using your oars. Similarly Leadership is also an interplay of several forces which establish how good or bad navigator you are. By setting the direction and pace, the leader establishes his command and control over the given conditions. It also shows his confidence and competence in a given situation. He has to lead himself; a function that can not be delegated and simultaneously also identify who can do the critical tasks that constitute leadership activities.

When you lead the ship yourself it means that

    a. You take control of key functions.
    b. Based on sea conditions make mid course corrections.
    c. You own it 100% percent. You are responsible for the good things that happen as well as the pit falls you come across.

Leadership like rowing a boat is a conscious effort. If you have to cross a flowing river, you need to constantly move your oars otherwise you stand to be drifted away with the currents. **Organisations too are like ships in oceans with strong currents. If it does not keep the engines on and navigate in right direction, the ship can never reach its destination.** By staying ahead and providing lead, the leader also provides direction, apart from setting the pace at which to move ahead. It's also about taking calculated risks on the chosen path.

In governmental organisations, as a rule such confidence evolves out of the position or the post a person occupies. He may be a very good boss as a Director Industries but may become mediocre when posted as Director Agriculture. True leaders, having the core intrinsic qualities should be able to perform as efficiently if not better on either of these or on any other job. All positions provide civil servants an authority to take decisions. These decisions help in building up confidence in the organisation. Taking lead is like peeping the head out, it also means taking the well calculated risks. It is an act which you can not delegate. You got to do it yourself. It means one is proactive, creating situations rather be driven by them. As a leader you should be authentic, that is a difficult job but so is leadership. You should be what you seems to be.

Leading the way – Government organisations must ensure that their leaders have the right skills to perform their tasks. The organisational heads, team leaders not only have to possess the necessary skills but be able to lead and manage teams working in different districts or states or regions in different offices. It needs very strong, effective and flexible leaders. It should be a key concern of senior executives to develop future leaders. This is an area where government organisations are weak and it is very apparent in their performance also. Developing other leaders in the organisation is one of the hallmarks of a successful organisation. One can see that in such organisations:

1. There is an active involvement of senior leadership.
2. Focus is given to talent.
3. Right programme is put in place and used effectively.

Public sector organisations have to deliver with quality and efficiency. It is thus very essential that things are done in the best possible way. It calls for constant innovation at all levels.

Life is like sailing. You can use any wind to go in any direction.
ROBERT BRAULT

The art of leadership is saying no, not yes. It is very easy to say yes.
TONY BLAIR

Leadership involves finding a parade and getting in front of it.
JOHN NAISBITT

A leader or a man of action in a crisis almost always acts subconsciously and then thinks of the reasons for his action.

JAWAHARLAL NEHRU

Leadership can be thought of as a capacity to define oneself to others in a way that clarifies and expands a vision of the future.

EDWIN H. FRIEDMAN

The great thing in the world is not so much where we stand, as in what direction we are moving.

OLIVER WENDELL HOLMES

Man maintains his balance, poise, and sense of security only as he is moving forward.

MAXWELL MALTZ

Organisations too are like ships in oceans with strong currents. If it does not keep the engines on and navigate in right direction, the ship can never reach its destination.

2
Seeing is Believing

A leader should be visible – Seeing is believing.

The story of Mahatama Gandhi and his all powerful presence at all critical moments of history is well known. The Dandi march or The Swaraj movement saw him lead the nation from front where his action and words could infuse enthusiasm in millions of young and old alike.

The visibility of leader at appropriate moments gives confidence to the team that when the need arises their leader is by their side. Visibility is more than the mere physical part of it. Through the day to day decisions the leader is seen by the organisation and his presence felt. He is like the fragrance which is present but may not be visible in literal sense. It is also a communication tool which the physical presence conveys in verbal and non verbal ways. The body language, the verbal command and gestures indicate the authority of the leader. The physical presence and showing up at decisive stages is an important trait for leaders.

I am reminded of a tense situation in Ratlam, Madhya Pradesh in the year 1990, where two groups were fully prepared to settle score about the death of a person in a road accident. It was the timely arrival of the district magistrate and taking command of the situation with his words

and gestures that not only assured verbally on what would be done but the tone and the tenor of his conduct assured that he meant it. This helped diffuse the situation in few minutes.

In matters dealing with an emotionally surcharged situation the physical presence and the verbal/non verbal communication says a lot about settling an issue. It's like winning a battle, without firing a single shot.

3

Keep Pace

Leadership in all organisation can be defined as the process of influencing others to achieve a common objective, an objective arrived at by the team through consultation and vision process.

The National Rural Health Mission story of Madhya Pradesh brings home the point very clearly. The state for the past few decades had been performing very poorly on maternal and child health issues but in the year 2005-2009 the state not only quickly picked up the pace and grew, it sustained the pace in subsequent years and became among the top performing Indian states.

It may be reaching the moon like the ISRO – Chandrayaan Mission or finding a vaccine for Malaria, AIDS, Cancer or Influenza through the efforts of hundreds of researcher, scientist, biologist or it could be putting the complete sports infrastructure in place before the next commonwealth games in Delhi. **A leader has to involve his managers to put the sequence of continuous activities in place that would lead to one set of output or goal.** Leadership and similarly managements are continuous processes. These are not single step decision. So a leader has to constantly keep his team on track with sustained speed.

8 *Leadership in Government*

In governmental type of scenario where the offices are spread over hundred or thousands of kilometers and there is no continuous real time tracking like an industrial unit, maintaining the pace of a programme assumes greater significance.

The pace maintenance or keeping the momentum is a leadership activity. The leader has to see that the development project or a regulatory campaign should not fizzle out without achieving the pre designed end results. Pace setting

and gearing up gradually can be done by regular monitoring of the programme on various output and process indicators. Such reviews will throw up the causes that are slackening a programme. **It is through review and monitoring that the gearing up or pacing up is carried out in any office. It is a conscious exercise which should be periodically carried out.** It also reinvigorates the employees in the offices apart from updating them on the latest.

When we scale up a programme and put it in top gear, the leader has to ensure that the necessary track correction is also done accordingly and wherever other suitable modifications are to be done, they get carried out. This would ensure that scaling up and giving pace to the programmes remains in the right direction.

> A leader has to involve his managers to put the sequence of continuous activities in place that would lead to one set of output or goal.

4

Management and Leadership

Leadership and management are two different entities; leadership is on a higher pedestal than management. Management is the process of working with your organisation by effectively and efficiently utilizing the resources to achieve the goals. It is a combination of several processes. Leadership on the other hand is the process of influencing others to achieve a common objective. Leadership is a visionary activity as the leader has to constantly look for new strategies to achieve the objectives on hand. He should always have a basket of new agendas to look forward to. It is like simultaneously playing with 4 or 6 balls and constantly throwing up 2-3 balls in the air.

A manager on the other hand is involved with the various day to day small tasks. For example the state government can have a programme of providing agricultural land to all landless persons in 12 months. It is the government's political vision which will be implemented through the team of Collectors, Police, and revenue officials in the district. These persons become manager of the programme of land allotment and the head of the state becomes the leader, who gave this goal oriented vision. The team of managers would do the planning, organising and the monitoring activity at district level and further down.

Leaders need to create compelling visions for their team and then guide them towards its implementation. The manager – Leader role are different yet they have quite an overlap. All managers, if they strive, can grow to become leaders. Thus a leader has higher tools at his command intellectually and otherwise.

A leader has to take responsibility for the action or inactions of the organisation. It is like saying "THE BUCK STOPS HERE". Leaders can not do the blame game on others.

We all remember several instances i.e.

i. Shri Lal Bahadur Shashtri resigning as Railway Minister after a serious Rail accident that led to loss of life and property.
ii. Choosing to attack a enemy hideout in the face of serious threat to life. Like attack on Tiger Hill during the Kargil War with Pakistan.
iii. Decision to arrest an agitating crowd of 300 students, which has the potential to flare up into a major law and order problem.

These decisions may not always result in favorable situation but it is the test of leadership to come forward at such critical junctures and to take a decision either way and then own it and face the good or bad out of it.

Management is doing things right; leadership is doing the right things.

PETER DRUCKER

To inspire others, first inspire yourself. Inspiration is a guest who does not visit lazy people.

TCHAICHOVSKY

The quality of a man's life is in direct proportion to his commitment to excellence, regardless of his chosen field of endeavor.
VINCE LOMBARDI

One rule of action more important than all others is consists in never doing anything that someone else can do for you.
CALVIN COOLIDGE

The single defining quality of a leader is the capacity to create and realize a vision.
W. BENNIS

What gets measured gets managed.
PETER DRUCKER

Take time to deliberate, but when the time for action has arrived, stop thinking and go in.
NAPOLEON BONAPARTE

Behind an able man there are always other able men.
CHINESE PROVERB

5

What is My Current Role?

The leader and the team at every stage should examine their current role. In all organisations (including bureaucratic governmental organisations) we can place the employees into leaders, followers, the fence sitters and the draggers. The leaders or heads of offices have to ensure that the draggers and the fence sitters are minimized. These are the ones who de-motivate the system and act as bottlenecks.

As head of organisation the leader must identity his current role,

* Is he leading?
* Is he managing?
* Is he just a file pusher?
* Is he just drifting with the wind?

This introspection is very crucial for the heads as it is going to have an impact on the organisation as a whole. This is very significant for officers and leaders who are holding key positions. Their actions or inactions are going to have a bearing on outcome of state programmes. It could make or mar it.

The leader on the upward growth path must constantly review his position vis-à-vis the larger goals that have been set and reassign or redesign the roles for

various key persons so that all are focussed towards a common goal which the government has set for them. This realigning/reassigning of roles is not a cost intensive activity but it can lead to tremendous improvement in the end results. The reassigning and the re-aligning activity for the team should be done in such a manner that it results in overall synergy in the team.

> *I studied the lives of great men and famous women, and I found that the men and women who got to the top were those who did the jobs they had in hand, with everything they had of energy and enthusiasm and hard work.*
>
> HARRY S. TRUMAN

People never improve unless they look to some standard or example higher and better than themselves.
                                   TYRON EDWARDS

Nothing arouses ambition so much as the trumpet clang of another's fame.
                                   BALTASAR GRACIAN

> The leader on the upward growth path must constantly review his position vis-à-vis the larger goals that have been set and reassign or redesign the roles for various key persons so that all are focussed towards a common goal which the government has set for them.

6
Just Do It

*E*veryday we come across projects which were conceived, designed and sanctioned years ago but they never took off. The total cost of such projects would be several billions when we take the country as a whole as this problem is rampant in all organisations. We keep thinking, talking and planning but not getting started.

There is a famous saying

> काल करे सो आज कर,
> आज करे सो अब।
> कल में प्रलय हो जाएगी,
> फेरी करेगा कब॥

Meaning that whatever needs to be done tomorrow be done today for tomorrow may bring a catastrophe and you may never have time to do it.

There is a Chinese saying that

> *"the journey of a thousand miles begins with a step"*.

We must realise that none has enough time to do everything he wants in his life time. We always have the problem of shortage of time. All leaders must realise when to stop talking and planning and get down to work. **Very often we find that we get bogged by the problem at hand and get stuck. I have learnt that** no matter what the size of the task at hand once it has been planned and broken into small manageable activities, the execution should quickly start with whatever resources one has at ones command. One should not procrastinate too much about the modalities of getting started.

Year after year we notice across states that billions of rupees are left un-utilized at the end of the year and this has become a global problem, the problem of procrastination. The solution of the problem is simple-Just Do it. Begin the job and do course correction along the way. I have noticed that any project that has been passionately pursued has never fallen short of money. Government always has enough allocations to provide to those who are willing to do the job. We may be fearful of various things that hold us back but this fear will never go away by just thinking. We can all deal with it by positive action and see how quickly the fear goes away.

Senior leaders, bureaucrats, civil servants are often caught in this type of situation when a project has to be scaled up or a new programme is to be launched across the country. They get trapped in minor details and the vicious thought process results in inaction thus killing an otherwise viable project. As Rabindra Nath Tagore has said

"We can not cross the sea merely by staring at the water"

One needs to take the plunge and start moving. Actions only will make the reputation of the organisation. Just do it has emphasis on the action part of work. Some things that need be kept in mind are;

    a. **Start as per plan**: Too much time and energy need not be wasted on planning but once a reasonably sound and implementable plan is prepared, it be started immediately.

b. **Don't bother about 100% compliance**: A 100 percent compliance of all steps in a plan in a given frame work would be an ideal situation but such situation rarely comes. We may notice that some unforeseen event at some stage would upset the ideal plan. In such situations the key is to keep going with available resources & make best use of them.

c. **Do it with gusto**: It means putting passion into one's plans and doing work with enthusiasm. Such environment always has a positive effect on the team.

d. **Take charge**: As leader when you plunge yourself into a project, it is not a blind action the work is led by a person who can command and give directions, one who can lead.

e. **Learning by doing** – No amount of book can teach you how to swim. It is by actual doing that we learn the swimming. Similarly no amount of class room tutoring or reading can actually enlighten you are out the nuances of a real life work situation. There are certain things which one has to learn himself.

f. Over Planning can kill a project so the strategy should be to keep learning, improving and doing mid course correction. This type of approach holds good for typical development programmes, bureaucratic work and lot of similar actions. However, there may be other projects like a dam construction or a scientific mission where the fine details need to be looked into in advance.

If you don't like the way the world is, you change it. You have an obligation to change it. You just do it one step at a time."

MARIAN WRIGHT EDELMAN

"In writing and politicking, it's best not to think about it, just do it."

GORE VIDALS

"The whole idea of motivation is a trap. Forget motivation. Just do it. Exercise, lose weight, test your blood sugar, or whatever. Do it without motivation. And then, guess what? After you start doing the thing, that's when the motivation comes and makes it easy for you to keep on doing it."

JOHN C. MAXWELL

Doing what you love is the cornerstone of having abundance in your life.

WAYNE DYER

Do not wait; the time will never be "just right." Start where you stand, and work with whatever tools you may have at your command, and better tools will be found as you go along.

NAPOLEON HILL

"The secret of getting ahead is getting started. The secret of getting started is breaking your complex overwhelming tasks into small manageable tasks, and then starting on the first one."

MARK TWAIN

Take time to deliberate, but when the time for action has arrived, stop thinking and go in.

NAPOLEON BONAPARTE

"I have been impressed with the urgency of doing. Knowing is not enough; we must apply. Being willing is not enough; we must do."

LEONARDO DA VINCI

The difference between what we do and what we are capable of doing would suffice to solve most of the world's problem.

M.K. GANDHI

The way to get started is to quit talking and begin doing.

WALT DISNEY

If you're not making mistakes, then you're not doing anything. I'm positive that a doer makes mistakes

JOHN WOODEN

If you believe in what you are doing, then let nothing hold you up in your work. Much of the best work of the world has been done against seeming impossibilities. The thing is to get the work done.

DALE CARNEGIE

I never did anything worth doing by accident, nor did any of my inventions come by accident; they came by work.

PLATO

It's the sense of duty that keeps you going sometimes when things get very, very rough. Somebody's got to do it. And if you don't, who will?

NORMAN SCHWARZKOPF

Very often we find that we get bogged by the problem at hand and get stuck. I have learnt that no matter what the size of the task at hand once it has been planned and broken into small manageable activities, the execution should quickly start with whatever resources one has at ones command.

7

Monitor, Monitor and Monitor

*L*et me begin by narrating what happened with me in October 2000. I was posted as Divisional commissioner in Bilaspus. In one of the annual reviews by the then Agriculture Production Commissioner Shri Shankar Narayanan, it came out that the performance of the division was among the poorest in the state. He motivated me to pay attention to the issue of distribution of agricultural implements. I caught on and started monitoring on a fortnightly basis with all concerned departments. The results were amazing. Monitoring made us rise from the bottom to the top position in the state. We also showed the maximum % growth in the state.

Leadership involves developing some system to find what is happening in the organisation, departments and in its far flung offices. We all frequently talk about monitoring progress of projects. It is in fact an essential part of the employer-employee relationship. It also provides us a tool to check on the quantity and quality of work produced by the staff. As leaders in government one is expected to monitor the implementation of government policies. Monitoring can be done for a process, policy or a programme. It is an important activity as regular monitoring can help improve lives of thousands of people.

It helps organisations in the following ways –

1. Helps in assessing how various components of a plan or programme are progressing in respect of funds utilization and physical progress.
2. Helps identify various bottlenecks.
3. Helps developing inter sectoral coordination on a continuing basis. (This is very important in mega infrastructure projects or some other project which has been launched all over the state).
4. Helps in identifying what innovative approaches are being adopted by various branches working at field level.

Once a problem has been identified its root cause and the effect it is having should be identified so that concrete solutions can be developed. Depending on the type of government department monitoring can take different shape. Some things that should be always kept in mind are -

a. It is a key strategic activity and must be done regularly by the senior management.
b. Physical and financial monitoring for projects involving infrastructure projects is carried out so that there are no last minute rushes at the end of the financial year.
c. Problems noticed are redressed immediately or as quickly as possible otherwise cost over run and time over runs can cause serious problems.
d. Regularity of monitoring is maintained by the same person.
f. It should be regularly carried out at various levels in the organisation so that the same message is transmitted down the line.

Monitor, Monitor and Monitor **23**

In infrastructure and services departments monitoring assumes critical significance as these are the departments that later throw up bigger social issues like scarcity of water, out break of diseases, sharp drop out in schools, malnutrition among children etc. Monitoring of performance can help develop measures to evaluate whether the designated agencies are delivering services consistent with citizen needs. Depending on the task of organisation monitoring could be daily, fortnightly, monthly or weekly. But it has to be done.

Financial monitoring is very significant as all governments keep complaining about financial crunch. Budget is a very important tool in monitoring. It can help bring in speed in projects completion. The findings of the monitoring should not remain confined to the supervisors but should be shared with other officers in the chain. It can educate them and keep them updated on what's happening in the organisation. Monitoring is a very important tool for all Leaders. This is a critical function which they should not delegate. Monitoring on various critical indicators at weekly/fortnightly/monthly or quarterly can give valuable insight into;

1. The strengths of teams in different regions.
2. The challenges and problems the team is facing.
3. What corrective steps need to be immediately initiated?
4. Who are the persons who can be nurtured and who can develop to become successful future leaders?
5. What local level innovations are happening that can be scaled up.

In infrastructure and services departments monitoring assumes critical significance as these are the departments that later throw up bigger social issues like scarcity of water, out break of diseases, sharp drop out in schools, malnutrition among children etc. Monitoring of performance can help develop measures to evaluate whether the designated agencies are delivering services consistent with citizen needs.

8

Keep Continuous Trajectory Controls

The team is like a long distance guided missile. Once fired it has to traverse an unknown terrain with its radars and sensors sending back field data and the trajectory being constantly adjusted so that the sight of the target is not lost. **Continuous trajectory controls means keeping a vigilant eye on what all is happening in the organisation. Periodic monitoring provides senior management a systematic opportunity to keep an eye on what is happening at various levels.** The feed back received on expenditure, release of funds or inventories at various places can provide quick insight into what corrective steps need to be taken.

Trajectory controls gives a feeling of target in mind. All organisation, departments etc. that are meant to fulfill a public purpose must have broad targets and the organisational actions should be aimed at meeting those goals. The feed back mechanism also gives us an idea about the situation on ground. Mid course correction is an essential activity and must be done in all organisations. In the constantly changing economic and technological scenario it is very important to keep external factors in mind. Ultimately the governments are working in

26 *Leadership in Government*

systems which are dependent on various factors, the better mid course correction we have the better would be the final outcome.

Continuous trajectory controls means keeping a vigilant eye on what all is happening in the organisation. Periodic monitoring provides senior management a systematic opportunity to keep an eye on what is happening at various levels.

9

Consolidate the Gains

We all work to meet the deadlines and targets given by the government. It is very essential for all heads to have a good grip over the organisational affairs. Periodic reviews are a very powerful tool for that. This knowledge can in turn be used to consolidate the gains, which have been achieved over the period under review. The process of consolidation in a governmental scenario would involve the following:

1. **Keeping the motivation level high:** As the systems set in, it is essential that the gains should act as a motivator to the team of employees. This can be done by sharing the progress story with the team and cheering them up to move on. It may mean expanding the activities to newer areas or to take a programme to the next stage of implementation.
2. **Doing away with the superfluous:** All programmes and projects may not go along the route planned in advance. During the course of implementation it may have to be modified to accommodate the changes that have happened in the external/internal environment of the organisation. It could be change or transfer of key personnel, rise in input costs or changes in policies of the government. These changes would require suitable adjustments. It may mean

doing away with some components or modifying it in such a manner that it takes care of the exigencies. Government projects and programme very often come across such problems. Some of them are:-

a. **Rise of new stake holders** – This happens particularly in programme aimed at individual benefits.
b. **Litigations before courts** – This is generally resorted to by the parties who have not been awarded a project or by individuals whose interests are affected due to the implementation of the programme. Land allotment schemes, enforcement of ceiling laws, acquisition of land for public projects, litigations by environment groups are some of the frequently encountered areas of litigation.

Consolidation would help assess such issues and resolve by suitable readjustment.

Consolidation at every level:– Consolidation needs to be done at different levels by different functionaries. Everyone needs to review his progress and realign his resources to the objective at hand. **With every employee becoming a stake holder in the organisation, every individual should see the tangible and the not so tangible goal they need to achieve. The tangible can be the physical & the financial achievement whereas the non tangible can be the camaraderie, the feeling of fellow hood or the feeling of an empowered confidant team.**

Consolidation need to be done at the financial level also. This would ensure that the financial regulatory and monitoring mechanisms are strengthened and accountability enhanced. Thus the exercise of consolidating the gains leads to a smart and efficient system.

With every employee becoming a stake holder in the organisation, every individual should see the tangible and the not so tangible goal they need to achieve. The tangible can be the physical & the financial achievement whereas the non tangible can be the camaraderie, the feeling of fellow hood or the feeling of an empowered confidant team.

10

Pilot Locally – Expand Regionally

Leadership is a mind game and it has to be constantly explored how the next day can be better, more satisfying, more productive, or whatever other out put one has perceived. The gains made at local experimentation need to be constantly scaled up. In fact the gains of pilot programmes in new terrains can be shared the moment it starts showing conclusive results. It could be an agricultural campaign, planning a new road, designing water harvesting structures or a new health strategy. The strategy hold good for all.

All Governments operate on an extremely large canvas both in terms of area as well as the scale of operations. It is more so in our Indian economy where very large number of subjects relating to government have been divided between the central and the state government. Every day we come across some new programme or project launched in the country. When programmes are launched on a very massive scale in states, it is essential that various issues relating to the implementation of the programme are clearly understood by all concerned. Though it is important that the beneficiaries of a programme are also suitably made aware about the programme, more important is that the departmental networks of field functionaries at various levels get a clear understanding of what is intended to be done at the operational level.

It is desirable that all major national or state programmes be put to a pilot phase before it is actually expanded to the full operational level. A pilot project should be designed keeping in mind the following:

1. It should be done with a view to generate the feel of the ultimate environment of the project.
2. It should test the implementability of the project as per the expected design.
3. Asses the possible risks of encountering problems during a full scale launch.
4. To get the feedback about the project or programme design.
5. To verify the usefulness of various estimations.

The pilot programme is run over a small area or on a small manageable number of offices that could be closely monitored during the pilot phase. It should actually be an exercise to sell the idea within the system and to thrash out whatever problems it is likely to encounter. The results of such pilot can be shared with the decision makers as an evidence of the immediate value. It is also a way of communicating with the skeptics within the organisation. Pilots always help in reducing the likely risks, when we are entering into areas not explored earlier.

Some issues that must be kept in mind while designing a pilot project are:

1. Area of the region
2. Available funds.
3. Support from seniors

4. Level of experience & training of staff.
5. Time frame to complete.
6. The general work environment.

Pilots have today become the established practice in all major socio-economic development programmes. Agriculture, Health, Drinking water, Urban welfare, Education Social welfare, Land records department etc are some of the departments that always have some pilots under implementation. While preparing any pilot the planners should keep in mind the ultimate picture once the project would be implemented in full scale.

In government it is seen that programmes have a bearing on many departments such as Forest, Revenue, Power, Public work, Police etc. The assessmentof the pilot phase thus is very useful in finalising the final shape of project by suitably linking the participating agencies.

Expand Regionally: Pilots are a preparatory exercise to develop capacity to meet the larger challenge on hand, which is the ultimate goal. The lessons learnt help in allocating resources, revising time frames and also extensive sharing of information with the field staff and the public at various levels. It is advisable that data from pilot programmes be documented very systematically so that it can help in evaluations at a later date. It is also an exercise in developing public relations.

> The pilot programme is run over a small area or on a small manageable number of offices that could be closely monitored during the pilot phase. It should actually be an exercise to sell the idea within the system and to thrash out whatever problems it is likely to encounter. The results of such pilot can be shared with the decision makers as an evidence of the immediate value.

11

Communicate – Baat Nikalegi to Phir Dur Talak Jayegi

The present century is a century of ideas. It's ideas that rule the world. How quickly the new ideas gets picked up by public is the measure of a successful idea. It creates virtual followers. All active or passive actions are also ways of communicating with your team and your organisation. The leader got to realise this and encourage a two way communication between the team leadership and the employees. It also means bringing more and more persons in the organisational vision. If we look at the history of successful leaders, it can be seen that they were excellent in communicating skill. People would follow a leader whose vision and mission or goals are clear so that they know where the proposed change is going to take them.

In a typical government department like say department of School Education with an employee base of about 415,000 dispersed over several levels of hierarchy and salary at different places, there is no formal or informal way of communicating the organisational vision directly to the cutting edge – the teachers. Whatever perception they derive about various programmes is through indirect channels. Another problem in large organisations in government is that the periodicity of formal interactions between two or three adjacent levels is not regular. In such a situation the organisational vision, and the mission – goals remain a very general type of wishful statements that does not properly convey the spirit behind them.

Communication involves all manners of activities; All individual throughout the day are communicating in one way or the other. In the organisational communication our focus should be to convey credible and appropriate message to those on the other end. It is essential to keep the organisations moving. It may involve

» Requesting information
» Disposing information
» Influencing others to understand your wishes

In bureaucratic or governmental communication the problems one comes across are –

1. Inadequacy or lack of communication which leads to misinformation and misunderstanding.
2. Absence of focus.
3. Largely left to be done by written memos or letters.
4. Not spirited.
5. Non use of modern day devices like Internet, mobile, wireless or audio video system for clear and unambiguous messages.

Inadequacy of organisational communication takes the organisation to a recluse mode, what one may find in a sleepy, dull office in the by lanes of some city. Worse than this, it leaves the organisation at the mercy of local currents that drift it away from the organizational objectives.

Talking of organisational communication it is primarily the written communication and the verbal communications that the superiors convey from time to time. The secret of communicating well is knowing that how you say something is more important than what you say. Therefore, to create the greatest possible impact one needs to use the widest range of expressions available to you through your gestures, tone of voice and your vocabulary. Research indicates that our voice tone and appearance accounts for over 90% of the impression we may have on others. The break up is as follow –

- **Visual** – 55% – Posture, gestures, contact and the general conduct contribute to producing the immediate impression because our movements and facial expressions are deemed to be eight times more powerful than the words you use. One needs to be aware of their force and make sure to give them serious attention.
- **Vocal** – 38% – Using your tone of voice, pitch and pace makes a difference to how people interpret what you are saying. Because a third of your impact comes from your vocal delivery, you need to make sure it enhances what you want to communicate.
- **Verbal** – 7% – Your words may not form a large part of your impact but you need to remember that when the effects of visual and vocal wear offs the message is all that remains.

Therefore, while getting the message across to your team the body language and intonation be used appropriately.

Reading and Writing – Government work is always done through formal written communications. Even when a policy is declared verbally in seminars or other form it has to be accompanied by a written document giving all details about it. The day to day dealings of government are also such that everything needs to be given the shape of a permanent record of what is being said. It is important that we start by getting it written. Once it is written, the draft can always be revised at a later date.

Written communication is a more demanding form of communication and takes time. The draft policy letter or some other communication has to be seen and finalised by 3-4 different levels of officials before it takes the shape of an order. Written information gives us the opportunity to convey complex and detailed instructions in a proper structured manner. Furthermore it is much convenient to review what was written in a particular order at a later date.

The skill of communicating on papers to get people to want to read the document means first getting it written, then getting it right. With present day facility of computers one can make it more presentable too. Space, heading, paragraph should be regularly used. These are very effective substitutes for visual signals. They provide emphasis, interest and stimulus which encourage people to absorb the written material more readily. Communication, particularly written communications should act a tool to speed up the office work and it needs to be watched with care so that precious time is not wasted using Telephone, Internet, and Mobile etc.

Today work is growing at a rapid pace. The inclusion of internet, e-mails and mobile technology has made it possible that you carry your office with you. You can always have access to your team, staff and rest of the clientele through this. Telephone is an effective tool of communication and should be extensively used. It has the following advantages:

1. Instant contact.
2. You can communicate the urgency through your tone and voice modulation.
3. Available 24 hours in your pocket.
4. A very large part of guidance can be given on phone to speed up various programmes, by just staying connected

to 8-10 key functionaries under a leader on a daily basis; we can give very effective guidance to the team.

Mobile and Internet –

Communication at the speed of light: The expansion of internet and mobile telephone network in the country has already made us the 2nd largest mobile network in the world. This tool can be a very effective way to send across short and crisp massages to a very large number of persons almost instantaneously. This SMS service of mobile phones can be used to convey a large number of day to day decisions to various branch heads across large distances. Some example of mobile SMS can be

1. Fixing meeting – "the next review meeting of district heads is scheduled on 23rd January at 12.30 hours in the city office. The agenda would be same as was for the December 08 meeting. Please attend with all details".
2. Director, Departments of Women and Child, New Delhi has kept a Budget meeting on 26th February at New Delhi. Please attend.
3. I will be not be available upto March 31st.
4. Please send Ten Trucks to collect Coal arriving from Coal India rakes at Bhopal yard on 21st January.

I have used it extensively and found it very effective. Being a written communication it can be stored in the mobile memory for future reference or can be downloaded to the personal computer.

Who speaks, sows; who listens, reaps.
ARGENTINE PROVERB

If we are strong, our strength will speak for itself. If we are weak, words will be of no help.
JOHN FITZGERALD KENNEDY

38 Leadership in Government

Of all of our inventions for mass communication, pictures still speak the most universally understood language.

WALT DISNEY

Think like a wise man but communicate in the language of the people.

WILLIAM B YEATS

We have two ears and one mouth so that we can listen twice as much as we speak.

EPICTETUS

Communication is the real work of leadership.

NITIN NOHRIA

Today work is growing at a rapid pace. The inclusion of internet, e-mails and mobile technology has made it possible that you carry your office with you. You can always have access to your team, staff and rest of the clientele through this. Telephone is an effective tool of communication and should be extensively used.

12

Blow Your Own Trumpet

Government is largely in the citizen centric services sector. We can see its presence all around us such as the roads, power, telecommunication, sanitation, education, water supply, public health, pollution control, forests, postal, banking etc. Looking to the citizen centric face of government and local bodies they all desire that their positive efforts and development stories are widely transmitted so that they get appreciation and recognition for its efforts. In fact media is all about communicating the good or the bad of government action. There is a general tendency among officers in government to stay away from publicity or media. They would all like positive stories written about their departments but would not share information with the media. They generally hesitate in divulging or sharing information with the press.

Blowing ones own trumpet is an essential part of all governments. That's why public relations department is seen in all governments and public sector units. If one doesn't blow ones own trumpet and just wait quietly in a corner for someone else to do it, one isn't going to get very far. **Generally bureaucrats are a shy lot. They feel that if they peep out they would be laughed at, ridiculed or bullied by peers. It has bred** a sense of false modesty into them. **They like their work to be noticed, but are still a bit afraid speaking about it. In fact by not making their achievements known they are doing a disservice.** If one has some remarkable achievement which could really help people, but doesn't make that known, then surely his audience is missing.

In government audience is not merely general public, it is also making your own organisation proud about what contribution it is making to the civil society. So get out there and do it, you need to sing your own praise or of the department which you represent. Blowing your own trumpet is a positive public relations activity. It is simply communicating what you are doing and relating it with public. Some ways of letting people know are;

    a. Getting articles in press
    b. Radio news
    c. Television news
    d. Sending news briefings

It is seen that most of us don't like blowing our own trumpet. But if you don't promote, something terrible would happen – nothing!

Positive public relation always does not mean that you want to be famous but without it you can not make your product known. A natural outcome of that may be that you get attention. It is an exercise in communication by telling who you are and what you are doing. It is a way of establishing relationship with your target audience.

> *Life is something like a trumpet. If you don't put anything in, you won't get anything out.*
>
>   WILLIAM CHRISTOPHER HANDY

The very essence of leadership is that you have to have vision. You can't blow an uncertain trumpet.
GEORGE GALLOWAY

Leadership is an opportunity to serve. It is not a trumpet call to self-importance.
J. DONALD WALTERS

Generally bureaucrats are a shy lot. They feel that if they peep out they would be laughed at, ridiculed or bullied by peers. It has bred a sense of false modesty into them. They like their work to be noticed, but are still a bit afraid speaking about it. In fact by not making their achievements known they are doing a disservice.

13

There is Only One Life – Your Job Can Give Purpose to It

Our jobs give a purpose, a meaning to our life. It is an institution as sacrosanct as the family. For all who are in governmental or public organisation should be thankful to god for giving us an opportunity to do tremendous good to the society. All public servants, starting from the village level Patwari or the village Health Worker or the teacher in school to the highest civil servant in the hierarchy can make name and fame. They should be thankful to god for providing such rare opportunity called public services.

Our Job Provides Us;

a. Wages to sustain ourselves.
b. An opportunity to serve public at large.
c. An opportunity to play a bigger role in the development process.
d. An avenue for self growth and self actualization of ours dreams in this life time.

Through this service to community, our organisations give us a choice to take a route that could take us to new heights in the social ladders, be it

1. Being the President of India (from a Scientist).
2. Being the Prime Minister of India (from a University Professor).
3. Being Anna Hazare (from an army Truck driver to social activist).
4. Taking a future role as policy maker.
5. Being a Member of Parliament or Legislative Assembly (from a public servant).

Public Services – An Opportunity to Serve

What is the importance of a government job, more so for those who are in leadership position? What is the tangible and the intangible that holds in place thousand of civil servants and million of other functionaries. There are about 3 million central govt. employees working in various public sector units and in central government set up including railways which has the distinction of being the largest employer in the world? It may be worthwhile to mention that this number of public servants has declined from 3.8 million to 2.8 million in the past 10 years. Which means that the productivity in general has gone up in government?

Government jobs provide a unique opportunity to serve the masses for most of the core areas that touch the life of a common man are in the Government sector. Defence, External Affair, Urban Affairs, Agriculture, Law and Order, Power, Railways, Forest, Roads etc. to name a few. Government jobs also provide returns such as

1. Self esteem.
2. Self satisfaction.
3. Job challenge.
4. Working for a nobler cause.

5. Serving the nation and
6. Job security.

It also provides an opportunity to satisfy what in the hierarchy of needs is called self actualisation.

Public services in India provide us a rare opportunity of growing as an individual professionally and as a leader in a wider sense. We have innumerable examples where public servants from all walks of life have risen by sheer professional performance to become Prime Minister and presidents of this country. Prof. A.P.J. Kalam, past President and Dr. ManMohan Singh, the present Prime Minister are two examples. There are innumerable other civil servants, General of Army, Secretaries to Government, IAS, IFS, IPS and other officers who apart from being successful in their professional life have also got an opportunity to serve as Governors, Ministers and Chief Minister of states. These have been men and women who excelled in their carrier as civil servants. This also brings in professionalism to the institution of parliamentary democracy as we are sometime accused of not having any minimum qualification for political carriers.

Public services may not be having as attractive pay packages as its counterpart in private sector at senior level, however at Junior levels the compensation packages in government are much better than the private sector. Very rarely does one hear that a middle level or junior level government servant quits his job to join a private organisation. Pay alone is not the reason for serving with government. It also gives the individual an opportunity to learn in new areas.

The purpose of life is a life of purpose.

ROBERT BYRNE

To live is so startling it leaves little time for anything else.

EMILY DICKINSON

There is Only One Life – Your Job Can Give Purpose to It

The goal of life is to make your heartbeat match the beat of the universe, to match your nature with Nature.
JOSEPH CAMPBELL

We should give meaning to life, not wait for life to give us meaning.
STACY

My formula for living is quite simple. I get up in the morning and I go to bed at night. In between, I occupy myself as best I can.
CARY GRANT

Be glad of life because it gives you the chance to love and to work and to play and to look up at the stars.
HENRY VAN DYKE

Life is like a coin. You can spend it any way you wish, but you only spend it once.
LILLIAN DICKSON

If A equals success, then the formula is: $A = X + Y + Z$, where X is work, Y is play, and Z is keep your mouth shut.
ALBERT EINSTEIN

If you stop struggling, then you stop life.
HUEY NEWTON

Life is like a ten-speed bicycle. Most of us have gears we never use.
CHARLES SCHULZ

Public services in India provide us a rare opportunity of growing as an individual professionally and as a leader in a wider sense. We have innumerable examples where public servants from all walks of life have risen by sheer professional performance to become Prime Minister and presidents of this country.

14

A Visual Reminder – the Focus

All leaders should always keep the mission, the objective and the goals in focus. One way is to convert it into a physical object or a picture that is always before you, on your working table,

on your meeting table and the dinning table. For example – A Grow More Wheat project can be visualised by keeping a bunch of wheat shafts or a new coal project symbolized by a nicely cut coal piece on your office table. There can be various other ways to convert an idea to a tangible object. It really helps. By always being before your eyes it involuntarily makes you think about the project or the mission and come up with new creative ideas.

It's some thing similar to the saying 'out of sight, out of mind'.

15

People Quotient

One has seen Intelligence Quotient and Emotional Intelligence Quotient. In organisation such as government offices which are primarily services oriented like education, health, railways and agriculture, what is significant is the People Quotient of the leader.

A civil servant has to interact with a large number of people whose background may vary tremendously. In situation like a student agitation or a farmer agitation or a communal tension the success is assessed not by how many arguments were made or bullets fired to contain the agitation but how peacefully the situation was resolved. There are innumerable examples in India to illustrate how a people centric officer could turn the tide to his favour.

It is very rightly said that "winds are always on the side of the ablest sailor."

The people quotient is based on –

a. A deep understanding of the problem.
b. An empathic attitude
c. An ability to openly communicate and convey trust among people from his words and actions in past or while dealing the problem at hand.

d. An attitude that's inclined towards problem solving.

By consistently working with stakeholders and community a bureaucrat can develop his PQ.

16

Integrity – Something Beyond Compromise

Professional Integrity is a prerequisite for any leader. Honesty to the mission, to the team, to the resources etc. The evil of Corruption is one of the leading challenges of governments at all levels. Globally too our performance hovers between 80 to 90th rank. This is an alarming situation and needs action at all levels by all stake holders and not merely the public and the NGO'S who take recourse to the Right To Information Act to access various information from public offices. We can all work to make our nation a better place by

  a. **Prompt attention**; Promptly attending to all work that comes to us.
  b. **Cut down the barriers**; No matter what is the level of the civil servant, cut down the barriers between the public and the service provider? The multiplicity of levels apart from causing delays also breeds other unhealthy practices.
  c. **Computerization**; Wherever possible introduce computer to attend to routine type of work, like e-ticket, tele check in, ATM, e-payments etc. These and many such services have made the life of common man very comfortable.

d. **Decide promptly**; This is an issue that the senior leadership has to look into. It has been observed that prompt decisions based on well laid rules and regulations can be a very effective guard in checking corrupt practices. Prompt decisions also preempt influence coming on a delayed matter from other quarters.
e. **Pass speaking order;** Pass well reasoned speaking order, specifically in matters where a reasoned discretion is being exercised.
f. **Awareness;** Generate awareness that clean work is appreciated and that prompt services are for all.

Corruption if left unattended spreads and generate a sense of resignation among people apart from breeding pessimism and inefficiency. It's an issue that has to be vigorously dealt by all civil servants at all levels.

Public Service is a difficult Job particularly for the Civil Servants who remain always in public eye. The face of government – the government offices- is what the common man sees in his day to day dealings. The delays, the corrupt practices of all types pinch every citizen. Professional integrity at every stage and of every type is expected from all public Servants. Heads in bureaucracies represent large organisation and the ethical standards set by the man at top sets the ball rolling. It means being fair and honest for if one ceases to be fair & honest he cease to have a conscience. The Civil Services conduct rules elaborately speak about the norms of behavior to be observed by Civil Servants in their work. These should form the corner stone of their professional conduct. In the past few decades the standards have fallen at many levels but that is no Justification. The society demands standards of absolute integrity from all, more so from those who are at the helms of affairs.

Integrity is something that has to be consistently guarded & maintained on a sustained basis so that it gets ingrained in the day to day behaviour. It also develops mental and physical toughness in the individual which he can use in situations of adversity. A person with integrity would also be generally reliable under pressure.

> *"If you have integrity, nothing else matters. If you don't have integrity, nothing else matters.*
>
> ALAN K. SIMPSON

> *Real integrity is doing the right thing, knowing that nobody's going to know whether you did it or not.*
>
> OPRAH WINFREY

> *The way to gain a good reputation is to endeavor to be what you desire to appear.*
>
> SOCRATES

> *In mathematics, an integer is a number that isn't divided into fractions. Just so, a man of integrity isn't divided against himself. He doesn't think one thing and say another- so he's not in conflict with his own principles.*
>
> ARTHUR GORDON

> *There can be no happiness if the things we believe in are different from the things we do.*
>
> FREYA STARK

> *Never "for the sake of peace and quiet "deny your own experience or convictions.*
>
> DAG HAMMARSKJOLD

> *"A person is not given integrity. It results from the relentless pursuit of honesty at all times."*
>
> UNKNOWN

> *Integrity means you do what you do because it's right and not just fashionable or politically correct. A life of principle, of not*

succumbing to the seductive sirens of an easy morality, will always win the day.
DENIS WAITELY

Never give in! Never give in! Never, never, never, never – in nothing great or small, large or petty. Never.
WINSTON CHURCHILL

"To give real service you must add something which cannot be bought or measured with money, and that is sincerity and integrity."
DOUGLAS ADAMS

"Have the courage to say no. Have the courage to face the truth. Do the right thing because it is right. These are the magic keys to living your life with integrity."
W. CLEMENT STONE

"The man who cannot believe in himself cannot believe in anything else. The basis of all integrity and character is whatever faith we have in our own integrity."
ROY L. SMITH

> Corruption if left unattended spreads and generate a sense of resignation among people apart from breeding pessimism and inefficiency. It's an issue that has to be vigorously dealt by all civil servants at all levels.

17

Good or Bad – Decide Either Way

Governments do not exist in vacuum, and so is performance. It is built on several factors and one of the most important is decisiveness. All senior and middle level functionaries in bureaucracy have to learn this art of decisiveness. The act of taking a good decision or not taking any decision, for that is also a decision, if it has been taken after careful deliberation. Everyday we come across situations where matter of grave importance are found pending for decision. Bureaucracy is a Jungle of papers and rules where there are several ways of promptly doing a job and equal number of ways of not doing or delaying that job.

Talking of leadership in government, it is essential that all person heading key levels in government get the habit of deciding issues posed to them. It may or may not be the best decision but a decision taken with due prudence based on available facts in time will be much more appreciated than some decision taken after two to six months.

Being decisive means saying emphatically that the BUCK STOPS HERE. It may at time means taking a decision on limited information and may involve some risks but taking that calculated risk is what makes a leader. To be doubly sure one can put necessary safeguards in the office orders. All decisions needs not be good decisions. It is in fact a couple of bad shots that develops your expertise and confidence of taking prompt decisions.

To a common man on the street even the smallest of decision of getting his name added in ration card may be a big issue. To a businessman getting a coal mines block sanctioned for his thermal power station may be a big issue. It's all relative but it is important. Some of the ingredients of a decision making process are:

1. Study the matter.
2. Get the missing information by phone, fax or e-mail or even a verbal exchange can be sufficient (supplemented by a note at a later date).
3. Checking the law and rules (they have evolved over decades and help in consistency.)
4. Decide giving speaking order on why it is being done, either way.
5. Avoid vague or ambiguous notes, a reasoned speaking order is always appreciated.
6. Give copies of the orders to all those who are related to the decision.
7. Transparency is always helpful.

Life is the art of drawing sufficient conclusions from insufficient premises.

SAMUEL BUTLER

When one bases his life on principle, 99 percent of his decisions are already made.

ANONYMOUS

In forty hours I shall be in battle, with little information, and on the spur of the moment will have to make the most momentous decisions.

But I believe that one's spirit enlarges with responsibility and that, with God's help, I shall make them, and make them right.
                               GENERAL GEORGE S. PATTON

Not all of your decisions will be correct. None of us is perfect. But if you get into the habit of making decisions, experience will develop your judgment to a point where more and more of your decisions will be right. After all, it is better to be right 51 percent of the time and get something done, than it is to get nothing done because you fear to reach a decision.
                                               H. W. ANDREWS

A problem clearly stated is a problem half solved.
                                             DOROTHEA BRANDE

Life is like a game of cards. The hand that is dealt you represents determinism; the way you play it is free will.
                                            JAWAHARLAL NEHRU

Once the "what" is decided, the "how" always follows. We must not make the "how" an excuse for not facing and accepting the "what."
                                                PEARL S. BUCK

Decisions determine destiny.
                                           FREDERICK SPEAKMAN

Choose always the way that seems the best, however rough it may be; custom will soon render it easy and agreeable.
                                                   PYTHAGORAS

"Be willing to make decisions. That's the most important quality in a good leader. Don't fall victim to the ready-aim-aim-aim-aim syndrome. You must be willing to fire."

In case of doubt, decide in favor of what is correct.
                                                   KARL KRAUS

Talking of leadership in government, it is essential that all person heading key levels in government get the habit of deciding issues posed to them. It may or may not be the best decision but a decision taken with due prudence based on available facts in time will be much more appreciated.

18

There is Plenty of Room at the Top

Leaders should keep in mind that there is plenty of room at the top. As one moves up in the organisation one also grows as an individual with some core intrinsic qualities. It is this growth that always keeps the leaders moving up from locality to city and state and national level. Those at the national level have the option to move to global level. There are so many beautiful peaks available at Himalaya and at the top it's always a table top that can accommodate another person. One has to just show his worth and reach there. If not in one organisation he can move to different organisation at a higher post/pay. A leader has to ensure that his team realise that if they have the worth there is no one stopping their path.

In government, unlike the corporate private sector the promotions at all levels are done after one has put in certain number of years and has maintained very good performance records. Here the top position is decided by the man who is heading that particular department. Nevertheless an empowered employee can carve out a better place for himself among the leaders.

19

Bureaucratic Organisations – Positional Leadership

In government we invariably find that a civil servant, a bureaucrat or a Technocrat take up a job which gives him the status of being the Chairman and Managing Director/Secretary to Government/ Commissioner, Director General of Police/Collector in a district, Superintendent of Police, a Chief Conservator of Forest or Director in school education. These are positions that make the individual bureaucrat or civil servant head of that office or institution. Will he be a leader or a manager? In government it could be either. **A person is a leader or a manager depends on what he does and not with what position he holds. Leadership does not evolve out of the position of a person. It is related to what he does. If we do what leaders do then we are leaders other wise the person is just the boss of that office.** If the boss has created a vision-goal for the employees and leading them from the front by marshalling all the supplementary resources he could qualify to be a leader. The position of a Collector/Secretary/Director/Block Development Officer/Superintendent of Police/Divisional Forest Officer or District Treasury Office, District Education Office gives the person a platform to begin his journey to grow as a leader.

As head of office, a civil servant, is in a comfortable position to transform his role to that of a leader. Some of such examples in government in our country are:-

1. Dr. APJ Kalam, President of India and Bharat Ratna for succesfully developing the missile technology for Indian Army.
2. Mr. Shridharan, Chief, Delhi Metro Project who has successfully completed initial phase of Metro rail project in Delhi. Awarded Padma Bhushan.
3. Mr. M.N. Buch, recipient of the Padma Bhushan in 2011, former Vice Chairman Delhi Development Authority and Administrator Bhopal for successfully developing and implementing the master plan for Bhopal.
4. Mr. Anil Kumar Lakhina, former Collector Ahmednagar (Maharastra) who transformed the way Collector offices should function. Awarded Padmashri.
5. Mr. Singh, Collector Amritsar (Punjab) who led the project of transformation of the Golden Temple Complex at Amritsar.
6. Mr. Chandra Shekhar, former Collector Nagpur who led the urban reforms programmes in Maharashtra.
7. Mr. J Robeiro, former Commissioner of Police, Mumbai (Maharashtra) for effectively leading the police force against various criminal mafias.
8. Mrs. Kiran Bedi, former Commissioner of Police, Delhi for evolving new ways of Jail and traffic management in Delhi.

These are example where individual grew out of the boss role to take on the role of a leader. It is the sincerity of the mission of these individual coupled with the capacity to influence and lead others which has taken them to the leadership stature.

> A person is a leader or a manager depends or what he does and not with what position he holds. Leadership does not evolve out of the position of a person. It is related to what he does. If we do what leaders do then we are leaders other wise the person is just the boss of that office.

20

It's All About Political Goals

The business of government is fundamentally different from private or the corporate world. Whereas the bottom-line at the end of the day in most of private-public sector businesses is profit, in government it is not so. The goals in corporate sector may be producing more cars, watches, textiles, transformers, televisions, mobiles etc, whereas in government, both in central and in the state, the visions and the goals are much different. They are different in the way they are developed and also in the way these are transformed into actionable points.

India being a democratic country the political parties at the time of elections come up with their election manifesto. The government who wins elections builds its action plan along this manifesto. Similarly at the state level political objectives are translated into administrative action plan. Thus the vision and the goal are decided by the political agenda of the government in power. It could be –

- Rapid industrialization.
- Rapid Agricultural growth.
- Single point power connection to all.
- Free power to farmers.
- No taxes on agriculture.

- Waiver of loans for farmer.
- Each landless to get 1 hectare of agricultural land.
- Roads upto each village.
- Potable drinking water for each village.

A look at the election manifesto, which decides the actionable points, can reveal that it's all political. The political leadership would decide what route the development would take and what priorities are to be assigned. The managers or the administrators in government thus have a limited role to influence this stage. But this in no way undermines the leadership role that the office heads have to provide. Even within the broad political goals assigned by government there is a huge open play field for government officers. Some typical programmes to bring home the point are:-

1. National Rural Health Mission.
2. National Urban Renewal Mission.
3. National Rural Employment Guarantee Scheme.
4. Madarasa Modernisation Programme.
5. Sarva Shiksha Abhiyan.
6. National Mission on Sanitation.
7. Prime Minister Rural Roads Programme.

There are mission and programmes that have been started by the political executive but its implementation in field is decided by the admistrative leadership. **In fact the real leadership of a civil servant can be assessed from the way he leads his team to assimilate the objectives set by the government. There are lot many activities and processes that need to be carried out before those mission oriented programmes can be adopted by states.** The difference can be seen from states to states. There are states using 100% funds and achieving higher than expected growth and there are states which do not even properly take off what to talk of 100% usage.

The success of civil servants therefore is seen from the way he is able to achieve the state agenda in the prescribed time limit. He has to align his priority accordingly. It is true that our organisations in government provide tremendous opportunity to be creative and do something beyond the political agenda of the government. In fact almost 90% of all programmes and schemes in the government are programmes that have nothing to do with the election manifesto. All leaders can make ample use of the tremendous opportunity their jobs provide them and do excellent work.

> In fact the real leadership of a civil servant can be assessed from the way he leads his team to assimilate the objectives set by the government. There are lot many activities and processes that need to be carried out before those mission oriented programmes can be adopted by states.

21

Innovation All the Way

This is a word which we all hear in corporate world and the public sector. However, it is one which has been grossly underutilised in government. Simply defined innovation is "the process of making improvements by introducing something new". **The unspoken goal of innovation is to solve a problem. It is not just the invention of a new idea that we are interested in, but that this idea is actually "brought to market", used/put into practice, leading to new products, processes, systems, attitudes or services that improve something or add value.** Innovation has been studied in a variety of contexts, including in relation to technology, economic development, and policy construction. An innovation can be big or small, brand-new or just a bit different, clearly complex or seemingly simple. Continuous change is an important aspect of Innovation. Innovation is the ability to see change as an opportunity – not a threat.

Innovation and the organization; Innovation is one of the most important factors for an organization's development and growth. Some principles that organizations can follow to unlock their innovative potential are;

a. Anticipate and Exploit Early Information
b. Experiment Frequently but Do Not Overload Your Organization.
c. Integrate New and Traditional Technologies to Unlock Performance.
d. Organize for Rapid Experimentation.
e. Fail Early and Often, but Avoid "Mistakes".
f. Manage projects as experiments.

If we look around we may have to really stretch our imaginations and find an innovation that has been created within the organisation or by the organisations. We have often heard about asking ideas from employees or brain storming with the group members to evolve creative alternatives. Innovation is also related to lateral thinking and it needs to be institutionalised in an organisation. We may call an idea innovative if it is different from the traditional way of doing things, and maximises the deliverables in new ways and take the path of discontinuity. It should also satisfy the consumer needs. Innovation is a serious well thought process. For any organisation working on creative ideas, it should not be a one time activity or the activity of one group of persons. It is the inter play of various individuals and groups that we get the common ground idea, the big thing.

Governments are large organisation spread over hundred of Kilometers. Unlike a private sector unit which is comparatively small, innovation is a difficult process in government. Ideas often get killed due to the sheer complexity and size of the organisational structure. It is therefore very important that innovations need to be approached very carefully so that the idea gets acceptability across the department. It is seen that once the boss is convinced it doesn't take long to implement an innovative idea. Looking to the way government has proliferated into all walks of life there is need that the diverse government offices develop their own innovative solutions, discuss these solutions among different groups and find how to implement. New creative ideas should be continuously developed and implemented across all offices and as time passes the new idea should replace the old one.

Governments are primarily in the services sector. It is very essential that this vast area is tapped to make the citizen life more comfortable. Water supply, Power distribution, Sanitation, Traffic Management, Schools, and Health System etc. provides tremendous opportunity to harness the vast untapped resource called ideas. Some of the successfully implemented ideas are –

i. Mobile Hospitals – (Reaching the unreached)
ii. e-passport
iii. e-ticket
iv. Automatic up gradation of seats in train

Albert Einstein once said that

"Imagination is far more important than knowledge".

When we indulge in imagination we release the creative power of our mind. The scientists say that a mind is used only less than 10% by human beings. This massive store house of our mind if used properly can throw up newer ways to solve the innumerable issues that keep cropping up in our day to day administration. Every one has this hidden innovative power, one has to just stir it up and use it.

Innovations are generally seen as a top down activity; however a visit to the villages can reveal the hidden creativity of the human mind silently at work in all walks of life such as agricultural tools, water harvesting, crop management practices, processing, home building materials etc. The point is that innovative ideas should be promoted at all levels and allowed to nurture and develop. We should promote the spirit of innovativeness among our employees and their team leaders. Constant innovation in work also keeps the staff suitably charged up and motivated.

Innovations are powered by management. The management's main task is to create within the organization a culture of innovation which will empower workers to think creatively, collaborate on ideas and contribute their ideas to the company.

The people, tools and techniques for generating ideas are the motor that drives the innovation process. The more successful an idea management programme is, the more ideas it will generate. As a result, you need an efficient quality control system. At the same time, it is also important to retain flexibility in the system. If an idea is a winner, it is often wise to "run with it" immediately, before others pick it up.

> *Innovation has nothing to do with how many R&D dollars you have – it's not about money. It's about the people you have, how you're led, and how much you get it.*
>
> STEVE JOBS

> *"Innovation is the ability to see change as an opportunity – not a threat"*
>
> ALBERT EINSTEIN

> *"Just as energy is the basis of life itself, and ideas the source of innovation, so is innovation the vital spark of all human change, improvement and progress"*
>
> TED LEVITTS

> *"Never before in history has innovation offered promise of so much to so many in so short a time."*
>
> BILL GATES

"The five essential entrepreneurial skills for success are concentration, discrimination, organization, innovation and communication."
MICHAEL FARADAY

Innovation distinguishes between a leader and a follower.
STEVE JOBS

Just as energy is the basis of life itself and ideas the source of innovation, so is innovation the vital spark of all human change, improvement and progress.
THEODORE LEVITT

Creativity is thinking up new things. Innovation is doing new things.
THEODORE LEVITT

When you innovate, you've got to be prepared for everyone telling you you're nuts.
LARRY ELLISON

> The unspoken goal of innovation is to solve a problem. It is not just the invention of a new idea that we are interested in, but that this idea is actually "brought to market", used/put into practice, leading to new products, processes, systems, attitudes or services that improve something or add value.

22

The Buck Stops Here – Provide Solution to the Organisational Problems

A leader's job is not a job of some one enjoying the perks and powers that go with the leadership. You would find people thronging around leaders. One reason is that the followers get their powers from their leader. By aligning themselves with the high and the mighty they also get empowered. Apart from being the source of power, a leader has to solve problems which his followers pose to him on a day to day basis.

In government the subordinate offices pose all types of problems. It could be administrative, professional, personal or financial. A leader should be good at solving such problems. **A large number of problems in government relate to their profession and the leader who is good at human resource management can easily get over them. His professional competency or experience in that particular sphere helps him addressing them better. By solving problems of his team member and subordinates, the leader develops the faith of his team, apart from himself growing as a leader.** Problem solving is a serious activity at the personal and professional level and it shows the empathic approach of the bureaucratic leader.

Problem solving is also an exercise in communication. What are the types of problems the employees are facing and what is the preparedness of the organisation to deal with them. It helps in organisational growth. It is also reiterating that the BUCK STOPS HERE. That who is the leader in the organisation on whom his team can fall back for solutions and who can put an end to the endless chain of problem solving.

Problems usually involve questions or issues which contain doubt, difficulty or uncertainty. There can be other situations where a person can also become a problem due to lack of having the desired initiative. No organisation is free from problem and the bigger the organisation more complex would be the problem. This is particularly true for large organisation or departments in government. Problems don't present themselves in straight forward manner. You have to actually mill around with the system and then realise, what the problem is. It may be at one place but its impact would be seen at some other place.

Take the case of poor performance in vaccination programme in some states. It may be seen that the problem has been compounded by lack of funds, manpower availability, logistics, publicity etc. One may feel lost where to start with but getting into the details of it would reveal that only one or two are the critical factors, which if dealt properly would set the system right or it could even be poor team leader, who with all the resources is not able to deliver

Problems can either creep slowly or may appear like a thunderbolt. In public service one can find a plethora of issues which you may be seeing as a problem but it has not been resolved by those who need to. In government there can be various reasons for that such as,

1. Attending to the problem may open up some bigger problems. So it is better to keep it wrapped.

2. It may mean fixing responsibility on some one for non performance and take action, an unpleasant decision to take.
3. The problem is fraught with political overtones and it is difficult to redress it without handling the political aspect of it.
4. By raising the problem you come in the line of fire because now you have to address it.
5. In the absence of suitable monitoring and review mechanism the senior officials are not aware of the problems brewing in the organisation.
6. Absence of administrative and financial infrastructure to address the problem.

Who will bell the cat? Wishful thinking that the problem will go away doesn't happen, rather it gets worse. As leader, it is not significant whose fault has caused the problem, what is important is that once a problem has been noticed how you solve it and move ahead. Problems at their initial stage may need a small investment of energy and resource to correct it but once it crosses the threshold and becomes a menace you also need to pool all your efforts to deal with it.

Generally in every day public life we find the nation gripped by one agitation or the other. These agitations going to streets create newer problems to be dealt by use of force leading to casualties and adding fuel to already existing fire. It may also turn worse as we have seen in anti reservation agitation. Then it becomes a mere fire fighting exercise.

All problem solving involves a degree of uncertainty because in order to solve them, decisions have to be made. One can not be too sure that these decisions would solve the problem. Each situation is peculiar and will need a case to case solution. Some time it may be prudent not to take any decision and let

The Buck Stops Here – Provide Solution ... Problems **73**

the problem die its natural death. It is always better to deal the problem in a well thought manner and not let it drift away. One may not arrive at a solution but it would definitely take you closer to solution. It has been repeatedly observed that a proactive approach to problem solving always helps and for leaders in administration it is their essential responsibility to redness them.

> A large number of problems in government relate to their profession and the leader who is good at human resource management can easily get over them. His professional competency or experience in that particular sphere helps him addressing them better. By solving problems of his team member and subordinates, the leader develops the faith of his team apart from himself growing as a leader.

23

Leaders – We All Need Them

Leaders – every one talks about them. From the village level agriculture development officer and Patwari to the district official and senior heads of department and secretaries to government at all levels he is under attack. It is presumed that the bureaucrats have it but there is a feeling at all levels that there is a need to increase its role in governmental functioning in all possible manners. In the traditional sense we all talk of political leadership like that provided by Mahatma Gandhi, Nehru, Sardar Patel, Lal Bahadur Shastri, B.C. Roy, Kamraj, Indira Gandhi and Atal Bihari Vajpayee who were visionaries who led the nation at very crucial stages. It helped us in developing a great nation like India. If we see the past twenty years or so there seems to have fallen a serious crisis of governance, that is the organisations are not able to come up to the expectations of the common citizen or the elected political leadership.

The bureaucratic leadership, in largely government driven controlled system, is very crucial for healthy growth of the organisations. It is the leadership that gives a vision around which the organisation is mobilised. Those senior officials in government who are heading Block, District, State and National level organisations have a great responsibility. These energetic and vibrant civil servants can bring about the transformation which is the most needed thing in government. We need leaders from villages to the state level playing their own significant roles and at times changing roles from leaders to follower and vice versa.

As the nation grows and more departments are added to address newer issues, the governance becomes more complex. It means more offices, more employees and more issues. These situations demand that the leadership grows and extends to the subordinate offices with greater responsibilities. However, experience indicates that the expansion of employees' base does not necessarily mean that the overall effectiveness of the organisation would increase. The most recent example had been the submission of the report of the 6th Pay Commission which has recommended pay hike at different level of government employees. We read criticism in news papers that more pay does not necessarily mean increase in efficiency. One can observe that the hours for which a person is paid and the time he puts in to do the assigned jobs do not match. This is a failure of bureaucratic leadership who are unable to get the work done or give employees a really captivating vision or goal.

Today we are living in a rapidly changing scenario. The dominant private sector and the corporate world have infused new ideas and energy into their companies converting them from state level units to truly multi national companies, Tata, Ambanies, Mittal, Wipro, Birla, Infosys, etc. are few examples. These times need the bureaucracy in State and Center to rise and capture this growth wave. It will need organisational heads with vision, dedication and energy coupled with appropriate tools to lead their organisations from front. It is through such transformational interventions that any organisation can achieve quantum growth.

Leadership in present times is controlled by a few. In complex and gigantic democracies like India this asset which is inherent to all human minds needs to be nurtured and made accessible to all. All employees can use it in various manners in their respective domains.

Where have All the Leaders Gone

Year after year we find various national news magazine, carrying out various surveys to identify great Indian leaders who have helped the nation achieve progress by their contribution. The April 21st, 2008 issue of India Today magazine has identified 60 greatest Indians of the 20th Century. These are men and women who shaped modern India and devised institutions that protect our freedom. The choice of 60 persons, 60 years post independence, is an interesting list. Not a single civil servant finds place in this list. The list figures 16 Politician, 4 Film Stars, 4 Singers, 8 Scientist, 5 Literary figures, 3 Musicians, and 3 Businessman. The list is interesting in the sense that it gives an insight into what the 21st Century Indian mind thinks. These are the persons whom the voters feel that they had a role in carving the larger picture called India. Why is it so that a vibrant democracy comprising of more than 1 billion did not find one person worth mentioning from the government employees that constitute about 3 million strong numbers. Can this sizeable work force not throw up some thinker who could be called a leader? Barring Field Marshal Manaksha, and Statistitian Mahanbolis and 8 Scientists, who are not bureaucrats in strict sense, none from the public servants appears in this list of honours.

> These times need the bureaucracy in State and Center to rise and capture this growth wave. It will need organisational heads with vision, dedication and energy coupled with appropriate tools to lead their organisations from front.

24

Leadership for All

Can each of us become a leader or is it just the man who is on a certain position who can be the only leader? On a macro scale it is seen that persons who are heading organisation by virtue of being the Chairman, Managing Director or Secretary have a wider circle of influence. Their position gives them a strong leverage to make things move and leader make full use of their positional advantage. However, **all CEO's or chairman – MD, Secretaries do not become leaders by virtue of their designation. They would be called leaders only if they do what a leader is meant to do. If they don't do, they are just the head of an office and not a leader. It in not related to the salary package one gets. A leader is an agent of change for the growth and betterment of the organisation.**

A leader should nurture and develop more leaders down the line and empower them to think and acts like a leader. This would mean that the team heads at various levels take charge of whatever is happening under their command. Such leaders deserve full credits for brining out successful transformations in their work places and do it with confidence that it is they who are responsible and not someone 6 or 7 layer up in the organisation.

How can we be leaders in government offices on a daily basis? We can do as leaders do by;

1. Taking charge of the allocated task and be fully responsible for it.
2. Provide solutions to the problem at lower level that keep cropping up everyday in large bureaucratic organisations.
3. Develop the team that can confidently take decisions on matters on which they feel they are competent to handle.

By such repeated actions leadership can be developed at all levels. It is the collective power of large confident professionally thinking civil servants that ultimately creates a work culture that is citizen friendly for which we are meant to work.

> All CEO's or chairman – MD, Secretaries do not become leaders by virtue of their designation. They would be called leaders only if they do what a leader is meant to do. If they don't do, they are just the head of an office and not a leader. It in not related to the salary package one gets. A leader is an agent of change for the growth and betterment of the organisation.

25

Anticipation and Action

One of the important things in administration is to have the sensitivity to anticipate problems and address them proactively. Every now and then we notice a problem brewing around us and one day blowing out of proportion into a major crisis. The Kargil situation, several major law and order problems in various states, a project going behind schedule or having a cost over run (Kolkata Metro rail project) are some examples to illustrate.

The problems in government can be of various types such as:

1. Incomplete projects
2. Shortage of funds
3. Scarcity of inputs for a campaign
4. Encroachment on government lands
5. Power theft
6. Increase in traffic violations
7. Cases of outbreak of diseases
8. Employees agitations

Administrators need to develop this knack of having their eyes and ears on what is brewing where, which can lead to problems. The feedback from news papers, public representation at various level or some emerging patterns during the periodic monitoring can clearly throw up signals. It's the duty of all heads of organisations to be vigilant and do timely action to douse the fire. Vigilant leaders are those who make a practice of being abundantly alert and deeply curious so that they can detect and act on, the earliest signs of threat or opportunity. In the present day scenario in administration this trait is in short supply. Organisations can encourage vigilant leadership by rewarding people who display flair for being vigilant.

Vigilant leaders are externally oriented, open to new ideas, seek diverse perspectives, listen to a wide array of source and develop broad social and professional networks. All those who are at senior position in public administration should be interested in people and listen with open mind while keeping vigilant eye on organisation.

> Administrators need to develop this knack of having their eyes and ears on what is brewing where, which can lead to problems. The feedback from news papers, public representation at various level or some emerging patterns during the periodic monitoring can clearly throw up signals. It's the duty of all heads of organisations to be vigilant and do timely action to douse the fire.

26

Quality – Let Our Work Speak About It

Quality is one of the important cornerstones of any organisation. It is not an isolated activity but made up of several components at various levels. Looking to the way public services are growing world over, it is essential that leaders should have an eye on quality. To give it a permanent approach some organisations have developed manuals or hand books to constantly assist and guide its employees.

Quality can be defined as anything that enhances the product or services from the point of view of the customers or users or the community at large. The public administrators generally have to deal with issues that are relevant to community at large. To illustrate the point there can be;

1. Guide to quality improvement for medical services system.
2. Quality manual for construction of rural roads.
3. Manual for quality improvement in school education.

These manuals can help in monitoring and improving quality at various systems. Quality improvement is a continuous process in all areas of public administration and none can ever say that you had enough of it.

Components of Quality and what is expected out of particular services need to be defined for each department. These manuals provide a useful guide for quality improvement within the organisation. This also encourages the leaders to integrate continuous quality improvement practices into its operation so that over a period of time they become part of normal routine. These manual are a very important document and should be developed by professionals in consultation with persons who use it.

While the specific activities may differ depending upon the nature of organisation, local, regional or statewide, the developmental stages can be;

1. Developing an awareness and appreciation that quality improvement is a worth while endeavor.
2. Expanding workforce knowledge and capabilities in quality improvement practices.
3. Integrating quality processes into daily operations.

Quality interventions are a leadership activity so it has to begin from the top. Some of the key action areas and its major components are,

a. Developing long and short term objectives for performance of output quality standards.
b. Identifying ways to achieve those objectives.
c. Measuring the effectiveness in achieving them.
d. Process management – With emphasis on maintenance of high quality services.
e. Satisfaction of user and other stake holders.

Just as a blue print is needed to build a house one should have a blue print of how the organisation or system will look once the quality inputs are made part

of planning and operations. Apart from lowering the cost and improving the quality of operations working to meet the needs of the people they serve, quality is something that the leaders have to drive from front. It should run through the entire fabric of the organisation. Quality is maintained and improved when leaders, managers and workforce understand and commit to users satisfaction through continuous quality improvement. It follows a cyclical process of Plan, Do, Check and Act.

Any plan to implement a policy to improve quality is done by putting the plan into action in a pilot phase and check if the plan works. Finally the objective is either to stabilize the improvement that has occurred or to determine what went wrong, if gains as planned for did not materialize. It is a continuous cycle. Once one round is completed it becomes the baseline for the next round. It is a never ending process.

In public sector and in the bureaucracy, particularly the secretariate part of it, quality is not an aspect much talked about. It is presumed that every employee knows that he has to give quality results. It is not necessary that the employees have the same perception about quality as the organisation has. On the job training on quality can be very useful in filling this gap. It does not develop in isolation and it is essential that the office team is sensitised about what aspects of quality we are speaking about and what end results it is going to give to the end users and the organisation as a whole. Specific short training can be very useful in bridging this gap.

> *"Quality is never an accident; it is always the result of high intention, sincere effort, intelligent direction and skillful execution; it represents the wise choice of many alternatives."*
>
> WILLIAM A. FOSTER

> "Quality is not an act, it is a habit."
>
> ARISTOTLE

> *Quality means doing it right when no one is looking."*
>
> HENRY FORD

> *The quality of a person's life is in direct proportion to their commitment to excellence, regardless of their chosen field of endeavor."*
>
> VINCE LOMBARDI

> "Quality is never an accident; it is always the result of intelligent effort."
>
> JOHN RUSKIN

> "It is the quality of our work which will please God and not the quantity."
>
> MAHATMA GANDHI

Just as a blue print is needed to build a house one should have a blue print of how the organisation or system will look once the quality inputs are made part of planning and operations. Apart from lowering the cost and improving the quality of operations working to meet the needs of the people they serve, quality is something that the leaders have to drive from front.

27
Working in Style – the Branding

Brand values are generally associated with various products which we see in open market. Public offices provide what we call as public services. Some prominent ones are sanitation, telephone services, electric supply, water supply, public roads, public transportation, security and safety etc. Unlike consumer goods, branding of the intangible services sector is a difficult job. Nevertheless, it is worth the effort. The services can generate a brand value by –

1. **Each one doing its best on their job** – No matter what sector we are in or the specific task one is doing, it can be done. It could be constructing a new road, laying a new pipeline, sanitation services for the city, preparing note for a review meeting, writing a note on the file or any other activity like making a power point presentation. **It will have a positive effect in the organisation.**
2. **Let diversity prevail** – Today organisations have to do innumerable activities that need support of a large team of experts from Human Resource/Information Technology/Accounts and finance etc. Let each of

them show their best potentials. This can be done by promoting decentralised decision making culture.
3. **Be People Centric** – Public services are all about people. It is for the people and by the people. This should speak across the organisation in the deliverance of services, in public dealing, in communications and conversations and in reaching out.
4. **Benchmark the practices** – All organisations should bench mark whatever they are delivering or producing. The bench marking of services be done keeping in mind that the organisation has to reach to better levels.

28

See the Big Picture and Share it

Leadership is a visioning exercise. A big dream that can be realised with the available resource. We are generally bogged down by the office routine and the hustle and bustle associated with it. This chaos does not give us the opportunity to dream, create a vision and see the big picture. Leaders will have to build the big pictures by pooling in the innovative and creative mind of their colleagues. The big organisational picture should be dreamt keeping in mind how the scenario would look after 2, 4, 10, 20 years due to the intervention or the strategic changes being introduced today.

29

Time Matters

All leaders need to balance their times between the various key priority areas. It is through managing our time that we manage our lives or work. Bureaucrats have to work for long hours in office that may at the end of the day end up in neglecting some key areas. **All Civil Servants at all levels must pay attention to how they are spending their times? How the work is gets divided between meetings, tours & traveling, reading, writing, dictating, discussing, playing, reporting, thinking and family? None of them should be at the expense of the other. There should be balance between them. By keeping an eye on timelines we can put in a sense of urgency and focus into the work at hand.**

Managing times in office can be tremendously improved by following a few simple methods:

a. **Structure the day-** the day has to be divided between office and home. At home 6 to 7 hours go in sleep so one has just 6-7 hours left to pay attention to various family affairs. Leisure, children, spouse or personal sports, entertainment are some of the things essential to maintain a healthy balanced family life. At office the available 7 to 8 hours be structured in a systematic manner so that at the end of the day one can feel that he has contributed some thing to the organisation. Office hours should be structured between

1. Meeting public
2. Handling and disposing files
3. Conducting meeting
4. Giving dictation
5. Talking on phone

I have noticed in the past 10 years that by dedicating the time to designated activities you can increase the output many folds. While attending to one of these activities the, attention should be fully focused on that particular work only ie; If you are doing files than leave an instruction with steno not to send visitors, or phone calls. The same holds good for other activities too.

b. Strictly stick to the time limits – The sanctity of time limits be respected or it would encroach upon some other priority.
c. Use phone to expedite work – So many times people come to meet you on trivial matters that can be sorted out on phone. It is a tremendous time saver to dispose of such low priority items on phone or delegate them to some one else.
d. Indicate priority on papers and files – By marking urgent, today only, immediate, time limits 6 days etc, we convey the sense of urgency to the subject and put it in fast track. Such notes help and all staff should develop the habit of adhering to such time lines.

Time is a resource which is limited to 24 hours per day. This resource should be used in such a manner that at the

end of the day you find a certain Value addition to yourself & your office.

To realize the importance of time is the gate to wisdom.
BERTRAND RUSSELL

Time is money.
BENJAMIN FRANKLIN

Dost thou love life? Then do not squander time, for that's the stuff life is made of.
BENJAMIN FRANKLIN

Suspect each moment, for it is a thief, tiptoeing away with more than it brings.
JOHN UPDIKE

Little drops of water, little grains of sand,
Make the mighty ocean, and the pleasant land.
So the little minutes, humble though they be,
Make the mighty ages of eternity.

JULIA CARNEY

The long unmeasured pulse of time moves everything. There is nothing hidden that it cannot bring to light, nothing once known that may not become unknown. Nothing is impossible.

SOPHOCLES

All Civil Servants at all levels must pay attention to how they are spending their times? How the work is gets divided between meetings, tours & traveling, reading, writing, dictating, discussing, playing, reporting, thinking and family? None of them should be at the expense of the other. There should be balance between them. By keeping an eye on timelines we can put in a sense of urgency and focus into the work at hand.

30

The Well Prepared Leader

Preparation always pays. Whether it is the college examination or a routine meeting the well prepared always has the upper hand. Leaders in government and heads of offices have multifarious responsibilities and in that context it is significant that what is done is done with full preparation. Though preparation helps in all works of life areas of priority, some key meeting, an important interview, a briefing on crucial matter should always be done with adequate preparation. It means that you have:

a. The backup data on a related issue
b. One is conversant with the Rules and regulation on the subject
c. Is familiar with risks involved

A well prepared individual can meet the challenges with much confidence and determination than an unprepared person. He can also bounce back with greater enthusiasm.

31

Take Responsibility for Action

In Government quite often we come across a situation where one has to identity the person who has brought the organisation some fame. One would never find problem in identifying such leader for there would be several persons claiming credit for positive transformations. However, when certain development, lead to some problems one would find that there would be none ready to take responsibility. A typical example can be a train derailment or some other accident or a police firing that leads to death of some persons. One will notice that it would be a very difficult process in government to exactly pin point the person responsible for the mishap.

True leadership lies in owning up responsibility for ones actions good or bad. On several occasions we have situation where a certain decision did not yield the expected results. This does not mean that you hang the person who took that decision. The owning up of responsibility is a trait of growing leadership. Leaders should see that where a decision is not malafide or rash, they should evaluate how the organisation can learn from that experience. There are certain individuals who would like to corner all the glory but would find a scapegoat if there is failure. Such actions should be avoided.

Accountability is more significant for those who also have the authority as it is authority that gives, an individual to make thing happen in a certain way.

I believe that every right implies a responsibility; every opportunity, an obligation; every possession, a duty.
                                        JOHN D. ROCKEFELLER, JR.

Life is a promise; fulfill it.
                                        MOTHER TERESA

We are wise not by the recollection of our past, but by the responsibility for our future.
                                        GEORGE BERNARD SHAW

It is not only for what we do that we are held responsible, but also for what we do not do.
                                        JOHN BAPTISTE MOLIÉRE

Make the best use of what is in your power, and take the rest as it happens.
                                        EPICTETUS

Man must cease attributing his problems to his environment, and learn again to exercise his will – his personal responsibility.
                                        ALBERT EINSTEIN

A new position of responsibility will usually show a man to be a far stronger creature than was supposed.
                                        WILLIAM JAMES

True leadership lies in owning up responsibility for ones actions good or bad. On several occasions we have situation where a certain decision did not yield the expected results. This does not mean that you hang the person who took that decision. The owning up of responsibility is a trait of growing leadership.

32

Change the Rules – Know the Rules

We all hear the phrase RULE OF LAW. Laws and rules are the basic framework that holds government functioning in place in terms of consistency and impartiality. All societies perpetually remain in a state of evolution. In regimented governmental organisation like the bureaucratic offices at secretariats, directorates and similar other offices rules and regulations form the framework on which our system rests. In dynamic times like the 21st century when the changes are rapid all around, it is essential that the rules and regulations are constantly revised, modified or repealed to keep them in harmony with the societal needs. Rules are meant for citizen's comfort and not vice versa.

I am reminded of an incident in which I was called before a court of law in my capacity as District Collector to explain the position of the state in respect to certain rules. When I got the notice I was a bit surprised as I had never heard about those rules made way back in 1930's. On a detailed scrutiny I realised that those rules became outdated as the medical technology had undergone a sea change but none paid attention to amend these rules and they remained on the rule book in the same stage in which it was first implemented in 1930's.

Outdated rules, regulations and enactments are galore in all governmental departments. It is an area that should be regularly updated. A pro-active administration would always be a step ahead of time. The reactive type of rule making does not leave a healthy impression on public who expect their matters to be attended at the earliest. Revising departmental rules and regulations is a comparatively simpler process. Whenever such changes become necessary, it is always better to discuss it with the stake holders and the end user. Such open interaction always helps and a better option emerges. Once an issue crop up it becomes impossible to change such rules in a short time as it becomes a multi department activity.

A recent study by Health &Family Welfare Department on Health Laws in Madhya Pradesh has come across more than 100 central and state laws that deal with matter of public health and most of the officials were unaware of the plethora of such laws. In fact locating the main enactment and supportive rules became a difficult task as these laws were made several decades ago.

Rules and regulations evolve from some law. Such laws also need to be constantly put to scrutiny and amended from time to time. Such changes take time. It is therefore essential that the exercise in learning and un learning is regularly carried out at each level.

When you want to break rules in a positive way, look for the rules in the way ordinary people want them broken.
AMITABH BACCHAN

Nordstrom's Rules for Employees: Rule # 1: Use your good judgment in all situations, there are no additional rules.
UNKNOWN SOURCE

The golden rule is that there are no golden rules.
GEORGE BERNARD SHAW

You have to learn the rules of the game. And then you have to play better than anyone else.
ALBERT EINSTEIN

Imagination rules the world.
NAPOLEON BONAPARTE

If you work hard and play by the rules, this country is truly open to you. You can achieve anything.
ARNOLD SCHWARZENEGGER

There are two great rules of life; the one general and the other particular. The first is that everyone can, in the end, get what he wants, if he only tries. That is the general rule. The particular rule is that every individual is, more or less, an exception to the rule.
SAMUEL BUTLER

33
Bench Mark – Set the Work Standards

Benchmarking can be on various processes in the department that are measurable. Services of private agencies can also be employed to get this exercise carried out. While setting the bench marking from inventory to customer care, the best in the chosen sector be set. In fixing slightly stretched targets the employees focus should also be kept in mind and keep them motivated on a constant basis. Benchmarking is a well thought and systemic exercise which can be done by seeking assistance from professional bodies like business schools. It has to be in line with the main focus areas of the organisation and be quantifiable so that it can be regularly monitored. To illustrate, it could be;

a. Revenue collected
b. Cases disposed
c. Units produced
d. Land acquisitions completed
e. Kilometer of roads completed
f. Number of pumps electrified
g. Efficiency of power generation
h. Loans disbursed
i. Arrears recovered

Bench marking alone is not sufficient unless it is coupled by regular monitoring to chase up the targets and make corrective steps wherever needed.

Whatever is worth doing at all is worth doing well.
CHESTERFIELD

Acceptance of prevailing standards often means we have no standards of our own.
JEAN TOOMER

If you don't meet the standards, then you don't qualify.
HAROLD FORD

It is a funny thing about life: If you refuse to accept anything but the best you very often get it.
W. SOMERSET MAUGHAM

Hold yourself responsible for a higher standard than anybody else expects of you.
HENRY WARD BEECHER

We are what we repeatedly do.
ARISTOTLE

"The quality of a leader is reflected in the standards they set for themselves."
RAY KROC

"Let every man judge according to his own standards, by what he has himself read, not by what others tell him.
ALBERT EINSTEIN

"You can become an even more excellent person by constantly setting higher and higher standards for yourself and then by doing everything possible to live up to those standards."
BRIAN TRACY

"Set exorbitant standards, and give your people hell when they don't live up to them. There is nothing so demoralizing as a boss who tolerates second rate work."
DAVID OGILVY

34

Identify Key Strategic Intervention

Strategy of an organization is where it wants to go and how it intends to get there to achieve its desired goals. It is the declaration of the intention keeping in view the resources and the capabilities of the organisation. In this context strategic decisions make a long term impact on the behavior and success of any organisation. It is seen that there is a gap between strategy and performance. It has been observed that in most organisations the majority employees do not understand their organisation's strategy.

In government defining the organisational strategy is a job of the senior leadership at the state or by the head of the department. The strength of leadership at top lies in giving direction and saving the organisation from change by drift. It is taking steps that build on present strengths. **The strategy formulation is linked to the vision of the organisation. Just like developing the vision is a participative process involving discussions with employees, the strategy should also be discussed at wider forum of employees. It would help align the organisation culture, values and people to encourage desired results keeping the organisational resources in mind.**

Strategic plans, like the vision, are developed by consultations with employees who have to act upon it. A shared plan has higher commitment and gives them a voice in what need to be done so that they become stake holders rather than simply being at the receiving end. Thus employees can better understand what is being accomplished and can see their role in the large picture.

In large organisations like the government, employing several thousand employees, distributed over many layers, all layers need to be made aware about the changed strategy. This process be so developed that as it moves down it generates greater number of leaders. The total effect of such cascade effect would bring momentum to the change process.

Governments and its departments involve a large complex system of programmes and project each involving its own plethora of intricacies. Strategic plans in this context require that apart from planning, the implementing of the strategy it also need to be overseen by those who planned.

> "The essence of strategy lies in creating tomorrow's competitive advantages faster than competitors can mimic the ones you possess today."
>
> C.K. PRAHALAD

> I hear and I forget, I see and I remember. I do and I understand.
>
> CHINESE PROVERB

> "The one who figures on victory at headquarters before even doing battle is the one who has the most strategic factors on his side."
>
> SUN TZU

> "In action be primitive; in foresight, a strategist."
>
> EDWARD KOCH

> "However beautiful the strategy, you should occasionally look at the results."
>
> WINSTON CHURCHILL

"You have to be fast on your feet and adaptive or else a strategy is useless."
CHARLES DE GAULLE

Strategic planning is worthless – unless there is first a strategic vision.
JOHN NAISBITT

One step at a time is good walking.
CHINESE PROVERB

In preparing for battle I have always found that plans are useless, but planning is indispensable.
D.D. EISENHOWER

The wise man does at once what the fool does finally.
BALTASAR GRACIAN

The world has the habit of making room for the man whose actions show that he knows where he is going.
NAPOLEON HILL

The strategy formulation is linked to the vision of the organisation. Just like developing the vision is a participative process involving discussions with employees, the strategy should also be discussed at wider forum of employees. It would help align the organisation culture, values and people to encourage desired results keeping the organisational resources in mind.

35

Change – Do it Quickly

The past 2 decades have seen Indian economy in particular and India in general taking giant leaps. It is widely felt that had we implemented these changes earlier we would have been much better and higher up the global ladder. In all walks of life and all forms of governments there are always many identified issues, which need change, which would result in betterment. Senior executives and leaders at all levels should quickly catch on to a great idea and implement it. No matter what may be the size of the organization, change is one agenda that should constantly be pursued. When we say change it can be any thing we are dealing with, a process, a service, a product or the employees who could be changed by exposing them to new ideas by training and retraining.

All government system and offices represent a status quoist type of atmosphere. Change brought about by working on a bright idea would help all. It may mean

- » Reducing wastage of time
- » Less paperwork
- » Better product or services

Changes once identified should be rapidly pushed to its logical ends. It is all the more important in government set up as the top positions in government are transferable with no defined tenure. Once transferred you can not be sure what would happen to your bright idea.

Changes that would lead to organisational growth should be constantly worked upon. Let each employee in the organisation work on areas that need immediate changes. Once identified these should be quickly implemented.

Every one of us should identify internally at individual and at the orginisational level on areas that need our immediate attention. It is essential for dynamic offices and organisations to reexamine what all are happening inside and outside.

New ideas or new methods that have worked in other parts should be borrowed, copied or replicated and if you are sure about the idea do it quickly. **Generally government organisations are hesitant about replicating some good thing that has happened in other parts. We want to start afresh on ideas that are truly ours. This view should be discouraged as in the rapidly changing would it is not always possible that every individual will work only when its an absolute new idea.**

Change does not necessarily mean that the idea has to be given by the boss, every employee can contribute to ideas that would –

a. Lead to improvements in their own work place.
b. Lead to improvements in interrelated matters.
c. Lead to betterment of organisational performance.

It could be on the processes, the methods, the teaching or the rules that are happening in enhancement of the performance of the organisation or reduction of waste. Change – Once identified, be done quickly. DO IT NOW.

If you don't like something change it; if you can't change it, change the way you think about it.
MARY ENGELBREIT

When you are through changing, you are through.
BRUCE BARTON

They must often change, who would be constant in happiness or wisdom.
CONFUCIUS

Growth is the only evidence of life.
JOHN HENRY NEWMAN

It is not the strongest of the species that survive, or the most intelligent, but the one most responsive to change.
CHARLES DARWIN

Be the change you want to see in the world.
MAHATMA GANDHI

The wheel of change moves on, and those who were down go up and those who were up go down.
JAWAHARLAL NEHRU

Continuity gives us roots; change gives us branches, letting us stretch and grow and reach new heights.
PAULINE R. KEZER.

God grant me the serenity to accept the people I cannot change, the courage to change the one I can, and the wisdom to know it's me.
AUTHOR UNKNOWN

The only man I know who behaves sensibly is my tailor; he takes my measurements anew each time he sees me. The rest go on with their old measurements and expect me to fit them.
GEORGE BERNARD SHAW

"The key to change... is to let go of fear."
ROSANNE CASH

If you change the way you look at things, the things you look at change.

WAYNE DYER

If the facts don't fit the theory, change the facts.

ALBERT EINSTEIN

Progress is impossible without change, and those who cannot change their minds cannot change anything.

GEORGE BERNARD SHAW

> Generally government organisations are hesitant about replicating some good thing that has happened in other parts. We want to start afresh on ideas that are truly ours. This view should be discouraged as in the rapidly changing would it is not always possible that every individual will work only when its an absolute new idea.

36

Guide Them

A leader is a friend, philosopher and guide. During the day to day dealing of files I have noticed that a very large number of issues keep pending at various levels because to proceed further in the matter a subordinate officer has either sought;

- A clarification
- A guidance or
- Some other details

These not forthcoming the matter gets stuck at that lower level. These papers received in secretariat or the directorate are processed by the office assistant and then it moves up at a slow pace. This stage takes quite some time and is a reason for delays.

At the senior level officers can cut the red tape and multitier journey of files by deciding on the paper it self when it first comes before him without letting it travel the ladder of hierarchy. Such papers must get priority of attention as so many associated issues are held up due to this.

"The only guide to man is his conscience; the only shield to his memory is the rectitude and sincerity of his actions. It is very imprudent to walk through life without this shield, because we are so often mocked

by the failure of our hopes and the upsetting of our calculations; but with this shield, however the fates may play, we march always in the ranks of honor."
WINSTON CHURCHILL

A conductor should guide rather than command.
RICCARDO MUTI

"When we allow our conscience to be our guide, then our purpose in life will be fullfilled."
DONNA A. FAVORS

Discretion is the perfection of reason, and a guide to us in all the duties of life.
WALTER SCOTT

One of the secrets of getting more done is to make a TO DO List every day, keep it visible, and use it as a guide to action as you go through the day
JEAN DE. LA FONTAINE

"Your goals are the road maps that guide you and show you what is possible for your life."
LES BROWN

At the senior level officers can cut the red tape and multitier journey of files by deciding on the paper it self when it first comes before him without letting it travel the ladder of hierarchy. Such papers must get priority of attention as so many associated issues are held up due to this.

37

Love Your Self: Love Your Work

Our work is an extension of our personality, our core values and the wider vision that integrates us in the broad spectrum of government. You will find that persons who are not only well dressed, composed, prompt, have clean office; their attitude outside the working hours also reflects a similar person. When we love our self our total attitude towards things change, such as-

1. **Our dress** – We care about how we look, what we wear and its appropriateness to the occasion. We ensure that the clothes are neat, well maintained and match with our shoes, our hair are well kept & there may be a gentle fragrance.
2. **Our work place** – It would be tidy and orderly and there may be a flower pot adding beauty to the place.
3. **Disposition** – A happy and pleasant disposition in dealing with people.
4. **Speed** – Promptness in disposal of work.
5. **Worthiness** – Generally happy that one is putting one's time to fruitful use.

What we are visible to the outside world is what we are inside for we can pretend to be what we are not but can not hide what we are.

It is therefore essential that we invest in our self by loving ourselves and do things that make us internally strong, happy and satisfied. Ultimately it is this that is going to be delivered to the out side world. When we love ourselves we also tend to start loving our Job, which is our bread and butter and which gives a purpose to our life. This is a conscious act and a very natural one for we all want to look great and want a reputation of performer. Such a harmony apart from bringing happiness in whatever we do, also optimises our work.

The Grand essentials of happiness are: something to do, something to love, and something to hope for.
ALLAN K. CHALMERS

If you aren't good at loving yourself, you will have a difficult time loving anyone, since you'll resent the time and energy you give another person that you aren't even giving to yourself.
BARBARA DE ANGELIS

Work is love made visible. And if you cannot work with love but only with distaste, it is better that you should leave your work and sit at the gate of the temple and take alms of those who work with joy.
KHALIL GIBRAN

If you have love in your life it can make up for a great many things you lack. If you don't have it, no matter what else there is... it's not enough.
ANN LANDERS

Love life and life will love you back. Love people and they will love you back.
ARTHUR RUBINSTEIN

Whoso loves, believes the impossible.
ELIZABETH BARRET BROWNING

> It is therefore essential that we invest in our self by loving ourselves and do things that make us internally strong, happy and satisfied. Ultimately it is this that is going to be delivered to the out side world.

38

Self Belief

Whenever we start a new project we usually look at our available resources to determine, whether or not it can be done. One such important resource is money but it is not the greatest resource. Some other important resources are:

Desire: Everything that comes from life comes from the desire for this is the spark that sets the chain reaction, the desire for something. A fire in the belly that can not be put out. This is what we must have. This is something deep in your heart something that may be called destiny. Such a desire that is demanding and insistent can definitely lead us to desired results.

Vision: It is the grand spectacular plan that sees the big picture, the picture which attracts others towards it. By drawing up a vision we charter a path for success. It is something which you can see though that isn't there yet.

Persistence: Nothing in the world can take the place of persistence. Talent will not; nothing is more common than unsuccessful men with talent. Genius is almost a proverb; education will not; the world is full of educated derelicts. Persistence and determination alone are omnipotent.

We come across several instances where a person did not achieve something which other got simply, because he did not try longer. Not necessarily harder, just longer. So often the prize is lost because we did not persevere. Wealth, talent, genius and education are good, but can not and will not take the place of one who is tenaciously persistent. Persistence is a vital resource which all administrators should develop. In difficult times that we live today we will find that it is the persistent approach that will bear fruit. When the going is tough, as they say, the tough get going. It is a trait that reflects the inner core capabilities. It is persistence that helps in achieving our dreams.

Think positively about yourself.... ask God who made you to keep on remaking you.
NORMAN VINCENT PEALE

Put your future in good hands – your own.
AUTHOR UNKNOWN

Nobody can make you feel inferior without your consent.
ELEANOR ROOSEVELT

It took me a long time not to judge myself through someone else's eyes.
SALLY FIELD

Our remedies oft in ourselves do lie which we ascribe to heaven.
WILLIAM SHAKESPEARE

Doing what you love is the cornerstone of having abundance in your life.
WAYNE DYER

It's not who you are that holds you back; it's who you think you're not.
AUTHOR UNKNOWN

It ain't what they call you, it's what you answer to.

W.C. FIELDS

Whether you think you can or think you can't – you are right.

HENRY FORD

Make the most of yourself, for that is all there is of you.

RALPH WALDO EMERSON

If you really put a small value upon yourself, rest assured that the world will not raise your price.

AUTHOR UNKNOWN

We come across several instances where a person did not achieve something which other got simply, because he did not try longer. Not necessarily harder, just longer. So often the prize is lost because we did not persevere.

39

The More We Do – The More We Can Do

Human body has tremendous capacity to perform. It can go on and on for days without necessary food etc and at the same time it can perform much beyond our perceived expectations. **Strange but true that the more we do the more we can do and this goes on. Performance is not necessarily in the physical sense but in the intellectual sense also. In fact the virus of productivity is infectious and can rapidly spread across the organization. When one is passionately involved about ones job he constantly get new ideas to make things work better in various aspects of his life and work.** It is a habit that's got to be set in the body and mind system and once it gets rooted in, it's an endless journey of enjoyment. A journey where the work transcends the conventional watertight limits. It's a state of mind that needs to be set in each individual for it's is a win-win game.

> *We ourselves feel that what we are doing is just a drop in the ocean. But the ocean would be less because of that missing drop.*
> — MOTHER TERESA

It is no use saying, 'We are doing our best.' You have got to succeed in doing what is necessary.

WINSTON CHURCHILL

"I have been impressed with the urgency of doing. Knowing is not enough; we must apply. Being willing is not enough; we must do."

LEONARDO DA VINCI

Happiness is found in doing, not merely possessing.

NAPOLEON HILL

I do the very best I know how – the very best I can; and I mean to keep on doing so until the end.

ABRAHAM LINCOLN

Life's most urgent question is: what are you doing for others?

MARTIN LUTHER KING, JR

"Do not reveal what you have thought upon doing, but by wise council keep it secret being determined to carry it into execution."

CHANAKYA

"Success is doing ordinary things extraordinarily well."

JIM ROHN

Strange but true that the more we do the more we can do and this goes on. Performance is not necessarily in the physical sense but in the intellectual sense also. In fact the virus of productivity is infectious and can rapidly spread across the organization. When one is passionately involved about ones job he constantly get new ideas to make things work better in various aspects of his life and work.

40

Consolidate and Publish

Government organisations need to invest more into consolidating whatever is known. Every day we come across situations where offices or individuals are looking for old government orders for reference or guidance. Things are quite bad in large bureaucratic organisations where innumerable government orders are issued or clarifications done to subordinate offices or existing policies or procedure. Since there is poor house keeping about such records one forgets what was said a couple of months ago. This at time not only results in misjudgment it leads to other complications also.

Government offices are unwieldy in nature and such circulars which form the backbone of its working need to be kept in updated condition. This can be achieved by:

1. **Maintaining standing orders files:–** These are also called Guard Files and these are a compilation of various orders, circulars and instructions of permanent nature which are properly documented and kept in chronological order. These guard files are always maintained according to subject. These can be on –

- » Establishment
- » Budget
- » Planning
- » Revenue
- » Technical
- » Lands and Building
- » Stores, etc.

Apart from such broad classification each department can have innumerable subject heads i.e., in the department of Health there can be subheads of establishment like

- » New appointment of Doctors
- » Pension fixation
- » Disciplinary procedure
- » Voluntary retirement
- » Leave rules
- » Medical rules
- » Leave travel concession etc.

All offices should keep these circular, well documented and updated or a monthly basis. Whenever a new order is issued a copy of order be marked for the guard file also. Such standing order files should contain only the relevant circulars. Other miscellaneous correspondence papers should be weeded out from such files. These files should be kept for frequent referencing with the staff at section level. It would make them more confident and professional in their work.

2. **Publish Regularly** – Important guidelines and compilation of instructions should be regularly published in the form of compendiums. These can be subject wise categorized and widely circulated among those who have to use these in their day to day work.

These publications should be an annual feature in all departments so that a complete set of guidelines is available at the department level and which is updated on an annual basis.

> *"By academic freedom I understand the right to search for truth and to publish and teach what one holds to be true. This right implies also a duty: one must not conceal any part of what one has recognized to be true. It is evident that any restriction"*
> ALBERT EINSTEIN

> *"When you publish a book, it's the world's book. The world edits it."*
> PHILIP ROTH

> *To write what is worth publishing, to find honest people to publish it, and get sensible people to read it, are the three great difficulties in being an author."*
> CHARLES CALEB COLTON

Government organisations need to invest more into consolidating whatever is known. Every day we come across situations where offices or individuals are looking for old government orders for reference or guidance. Things are quite bad in large bureaucratic organisations where innumerable government orders are issued or clarifications done to subordinate offices or existing policies or procedure. Since there is poor house keeping about such records one forgets what was said a couple of months ago.

41

Know Your Organisation

*I*n the day to day interaction with various district officials I come across persons who have not properly seen their areas and they respond to situations on the basis of information given by subordinates. When some crisis situation develops in such territory the person has to rely on second hand information. Such decisions may lack the authenticity of excellence.

A leader should be thorough about his organisation, at least on the critical aspects that constitute the organisation. Unlike the private sector where the ownership of the organisation is distinctly visible and loud, in government this is largely vague. Not only have the leaders in government occupying their post for a short period their knowledge about the organisation is also sketchy. We have inherited the system which for ages had been running at a certain slow pace or rather drifting at a certain pace. Leading such an organisation is a difficult task. The Leader should know the what, why, where, who, when etc. of its organization. The leader here has little time at its disposal as some programme or problems would always keep the system occupied. Thus the learning process has to be done as an activity parallel to leading the organisation. We may call it **'knowing by leading'**. All heads of offices and organizations in government should therefore put extra efforts in learning and picking up the details of the job at hand, the area, the people, the resources, the leaders, the followers, the fence sitters, the road blockers and the facilitators etc. Knowing gives confidence to those heading the team and at the same time it helps building mutual confidence on both sides.

There are several offices that deal with issues which involve active networking with people. These are sensitive people centric jobs and require very careful handling of affairs. Here knowing the organisation is much more than merely understanding the basic facts – it is establishing a rapport with them.

Knowing is a constant leadership activity which grows constantly and develops around the leader and in the process empowers him. Thus knowledge of organization can be summarized as an essential leadership activity which involves knowledge about its;

1. People
2. Resources
3. Terrain
4. Core areas of work
5. Challenges and Opportunities

Gathering more and more knowledge about the organisation should be encouraged at all levels and among all sections of the organisation. It is the collectively enlightened and knowledgeable people base that would ultimately generate the critical mass needed for bringing about any transformation in the organisation.

> A leader should be thorough about his organisation, at least on the critical aspects that constitute the organisation. Unlike the private sector where the ownership of the organisation is distinctly visible and loud, in government this is largely vague. Not only have the leaders in government occupying their post for a short period their knowledge about the organisation is also sketchy.

42

Vision

We have all heard the proverb **"where there is no vision, people will perish"**. Most vision statements generally express an element of ambition. It is the unfettered ambition or being future oriented. Vision of the organization signifies a concept related to guiding an organisation from its present realities to a viable future. For any organisational transformation to be successful it must have a vision. This vision and Goal setting is interrelated. A leader has to keep the goals slightly stretched so that the organisation is dragged out of the comfort zone that it generally has a tendency to get into. The vision needs to be broad, continuous and should be capable to predict future needs.

An important aspect about vision is that it should be clear and also create a sense of urgency. People in organisation feel more motivated when they see the vision. It is here that the role of leader comes in, who has to mobilise the support of his team by sharing it with them. People need to understand the big picture and what role they have in its creation. Visions not only need to have direction and speed it should also have an element of momentum. If makes them realised fast. Transforming vision to actionable plans is always the most important stage.

For all high performing organisations and teams it is essential that they have a clear picture of what they are

trying to create. Participation of team in the visioning exercise creates alignment of other team members in creating a sound vision. The process of mission and vision is both a personal as well as an organisational task. It has been seen that organisations that have gone through this process get better rewards of alignment, empowerment, interdependence, innovation and commitment. All organisations must have a vision as it gives a focus to leadership. Those who are leading must develop a mental image of what type of organisational changes they feel are desirable so that it can achieve the responsibility entrusted to it.

In governmental offices the visioning process need to be done at the senior level with adequate dose of inputs from field level team mates. The vision of any department has to project a long term picture such as

1. Health for all by the year 2015
2. Education for all upto 2017
3. A fair weather road for every village by 2011
4. Universal coverage of electrification of all villages in 4 years

The vision would also indicate certain paradigm shifts which the organisations have to take to move on the path designed by the vision. In government the change of vision paradigm has to be done within certain constraints of the existing situation to bring about change in an orderly manner. It should include that,

1. The top management uses the process of brain storming to formulate the new vision.
2. Due attention is given to all possible relations that exist and interact with one another. The cultural framework of the organisation should also be kept in mind.

Mission are always a very much do function and it should have a definite action orientation.

Drawing up a mission in government offices is a difficult and time taking process but it is worth it as it gives the employees an opportunity to understand what that organisation is meant for and what are the products or services it has to deliver and to whom and at what satisfaction? **Above all it should have a dose of passion.**

One can keep in mind that the vision should be

a. Specific,
b. Measurable and
c. Attainable in a time frame.

A vision once carved out becomes the catalyst for a constructive chain reaction through out the organisation. The leaders need to test whether the vision is able to move people to action. It is not merely a statement, it should stimulate employees down the line and make them active participant who can later sell it to others without distortion. Transforming vision to actionable plans is always the most important stage.

> *"A dreamer is one who can only find his way by moonlight, and his punishment is that he sees the dawn before the rest of the world.*
>
> OSCAR WILDE

> *"Vision without action is a dream. Action without vision is simply passing the time. Action with Vision is making a positive difference.*
>
> JOEL BARKER

> *"Vision is the art of seeing what is invisible to others."*
>
> JONATHAN SWIFT

> *"The most pathetic person in the world is someone who has sight, but has no vision."*
>
> HELEN KELLER

"Effective leaders help others to understand the necessity of change and to accept a common vision of the desired outcome."

JACK WELCH

"Vision without a task is only a dream. A task without a vision is but drudgery. But vision with a task is a dream fulfilled."

JOHN KOTTER

For all high performing organisations and teams it is essential that they have a clear picture of what they are trying to create. Participation of team in the visioning exercise creates alignment of other team members in creating a sound vision.

43

Own the Organization

Some months ago we saw a host of agitations around the capital city of Bhopal demanding better wages for them. This was an outcome of the 6th pay commission recommendations on revisions of salary packages for government employees. The common factor among them was that they were all government servants and separately agitating against the entity called government.

Government organizations are sometime as non-specific as the government itself. Millions of employees who constitute various components of government do not consider themselves as the government. However, to the ordinary citizen every functionary of the system is a reflection of government. His actions or inactions are the impressions he gathers about what government implies.

Public services world over are largely functions that are done by the sovereign power. These are services that generally impinge on every individual in the country. Public Services therefore provide a forum for individuals to rise to their highest level of performance or fulfill a dream which they have seen, what can be called **'self actualization.'** This is a unique opportunity available in government. The power to be part of the transformation and on several occasions be the prime mover. However, when we look at the system in totality we find that very few persons view their role in that context. They tend to see themselves as working for some fictional entity called 'government'. They don't own the organisation.

The term own the organisation signifies that the employees see their role as a direct stake holder in the affairs of the government. The gains and the losses to the department, agency or a unit of government are felt with the same concern as if it was their own.

Leaders have to view things from a different paradigm and see as if they own the organisation. The planning, organisation, implementation, monitoring and all other aspect of work should have the bearing as if it is their organisation and so are the organizational gains and the losses. One can see that this paradigm shift would give the strength of an owner of a stakeholder – a True Leader. A natural outcome of owning the organisation is the element of passion one puts into the work and its passion only that can move mountains.

When one owns the organisation, some immediate outcomes would be:

1. The element of passion.
2. In depth planning on critical and important issues.
3. Concern for employees and the organisation.
4. Efforts to give one's best.
5. Working for a higher mission than just earning a salary.

Leaders in this frame of mind become real transformational leaders and any aspect which they choose is bound to succeed. One eats, thinks, dreams and sleeps with it. It is what may be called the Hundred Percent Leader. When one owns the organisation other things start to fall in line as if it was designed to support your moves.

In real life situation it is very much possible for all unit heads, field heads or in-charge of independent offices and Departments. One has to see the pleasant power of owning the organisation and as a leader and take it to the goal of self actualization. Your organisation in government can provide you that rare opportunity of doing it in that short time span available to you.

> *"Love does not cause suffering: what causes it is the sense of ownership, which is love's opposite"*
>
> ANTOINE DE SAINT-EXUPERY

> *The instinct of ownership is fundamental in man's nature"*
>
> WILLIAM JAMES

> *"What you resist persists. If you take ownership and deal with things that are bothering you, then, in the very process of dealing with them they very often will go away."*

Leaders have to view things from a different paradigm and see as if they own the organisation. The planning, organisation, implementation, monitoring and all other aspect of work should have the bearing as if it is their organisation and so are the organizational gains and the losses. One can see that this paradigm shift would give the strength of an owner of a stakeholder – a True Leader. A natural outcome of owning the organisation is the element of passion one puts into the work and its passion only that can move mountains.

44

Let the Office Speak – Give a Facelift

An organisation is a visible persona. The building, the furniture, the files, the office space, the internal and the external ambience and the staff in that office all communicate in a non-verbal sense. In fact this is what public sees and believes about government organisation. Giving facelift to any office is not a cost intensive exercise. A sustained initiative by head of office can bring about a sea change in a short time frame. Such as,

i. Smart employees.
ii. Cleanliness at work play.
iii. Orderliness at work place.
iv. Smart furniture (No broken shabby chair, table, torn curtains, peeling of plaster, dangling electrical cables etc.
v. Smart appearance – Curtain, window, doors, furniture, the files, the stationary.
vi. Courteousness in dealing with public

A smart team in a smart office can do wonder. In fact they reinforce each other. Once the offices have been brought to a certain level of orderliness, it should be sustained by a daily system of monitoring.

Smart Team-Smart Offices – Smart teams deliver excellent results. A smart person necessitates a healthy and active body. A body that can endure for long hours of works, which could be taking a long inspection in Jungle or a long note on file or conducting an extended review meeting at various stations stretched over hundreds of kilometers.

An organisation is a visible persona. The building, the furniture, the files, the office space, the internal and the external ambience and the staff in that office all communicate in a non-verbal sense. In fact it is what public sees and believes about government organisation. Giving face lift to any office is not a cost intensive exercise.

45

Make Your Team

"A leader is like the conductor of a 150 men orchestra, who has to ensure that they are all harmoniously tuned"

Government in most of the countries are the largest employers. Good governance is the key to good administration and success. It is a combination of various forces such as legislative, executive, judiciary, market economy, activism, regulatory mechanism etc. It is necessary that each of these activities take the path of good governance.

When we talk of good governance we have to talk about good leaders, who as head of the organisation like a captain of the team, takes the organisation to the next level. In any organisation there are certain positions or posts that are considered of key importance for operational success of the organisation, such positions need to be filled with care. Quite often it is observed that in government the selection to such posts is not made with care. There is a presumption that every one can do a job with the desired effectiveness. That is why we find heads of organisations being relocated without giving much significance to the suitability aspect of the person.

Some traits which should be seen while picking up a person for a particular job are –

a. **Commitment** – The head should have a clear commitment to the goals. His own commitment would provide constant food for thought for the team.
b. **Professional ability**: The person should possess the desired professional expertise to meet the Job requirement. If it is about accounts he should have the requisite qualifications to do the job or if it is about some engineering issues the must have the necessary degree in the subject.

c. **Capacity to perform**: It goes beyond the technical requisites and may mean the personal ability and the capacity to put in extra efforts that go with tasks of responsibility.

Once you find the person suited to the job trust him, support him & make him accountable. Support him if he gets stuck in a problem.

A leader has to ensure that the team can see themselves in the big picture. They should see that they are working towards a mission – a project which is their own. How? That is the challenge the leader address. This can be done by communicating that

a. The completed project would result in achieving a larger mission (psychological level).
b. It would give him some pride by way of constant appreciative strokes.
c. It would achieve a land mark in their carrier.
d. May get a pay rise or some other reward.
e. It could also mean a better work place.
f. A more empowered growth oriented individual and a resultant strong confident organisation.

> When we talk of good governance we have to talk about good leaders, who as head of the organisation like a captain of the team, takes the organisation to the next level. In any organisation there are certain positions or posts that are considered of key importance for operational success of the organisation, such positions need to be filled with care.

46

Look Out for Ideas

We have host of examples which are idea driven – where the novelty of the idea caught the imagination of every one to accept it, such as;

1. Ring tones in phone
2. Digital watches
3. Swaraj movement
4. Satyagraha movement by Gandhiji
5. Rent-a-Car
6. Landing on moon

These are all about ideas. In the day to day office work we come across so many ideas that can make the work place better or our job more meaningful. We should not ignore them, these be captured and efforts made to make it work. It is the consolidated efforts of hundreds of members that would ultimately lead to quantum change.

> *"Take up one idea. Make that one idea your life – think of it, dream of it, and live on that idea. Let the brain, muscles, nerves, every part of your body, be full of that idea, and just leave every other idea alone. This is the way to success that is way great spiritual giants are produced."*
>
> Swami Vivekananda

"An idea that is developed and put into action is more important than an idea that exists only as an idea."

BUDDHA

"We are prisoners of ideas."

RALPH WALDO EMERSON

"Ideas...They have the power."

NAPOLEAN HILL

"An idea is salvation by imagination."

FRANK LLOYD WRIGHT

"Every really new idea looks crazy at first."
                                    ALFRED NORTH WHITEHEAD

"The value of an idea lies in the using of it."
                                    THOMAS A EDISON

"An idea that is not dangerous is unworthy to be called an idea at all."
                                    ELBERT HUBBARD

"An invasion of armies can be resisted, but not an idea whose time has come."
                                    VICTOR HUGO

"Get a good idea and stay with it. Dog it, and work at it until it's done right."
                                    WALT DISNEY

47

Passion that Transcends the 10 to 5 Mindset

Passion is among the top traits of a leader which he has about the mission and goals of the organisation. It is passion that makes the world go round. **There can not be a leader who does not have a passion. It is what may also be called a JUNOON.** It is all the more significant in government where the performance of the employees is decided in a 10 A.M. to 5 P.M. work set up. Passion transcends the 10 to 5 mindset. Every day we hear individuals in government saying at 5 P.M. that they have earned their days wages or that their day has come to an end. Passion is linked to the wider mission that keeps the leader dreaming all through the 24 hour day, finding new solutions, alternatives or options to a problem or new avenues for the organisation. Dreaming when one is asleep and chartering new paths in the wakeful hours. It is passion that would keep the organization among top performers.

"Enthusiasm is one of the most powerful engines of success. When you do a thing, do it with all your might. Put your whole soul into it. Stamp it with your own personality. Be active, be energetic and faithful, and you will accomplish your object. Nothing great was ever achieved without enthusiasm."

Ralph Waldo Emerson

Passion is the genesis of genius.

Anthony Robbins

Nothing great in the world has been accomplished without passion.
George Wilhelm

Passion is energy. Feel the power that comes from focusing on what excites you.
OPRAH WINFREY

Follow your passion, and success will follow you.
TERRI GUILLEMETS

Don't ask yourself what the world needs; ask yourself what makes you come alive. And then go and do that. Because what the world needs is people who have come alive.
HOWARD THURMAN

Renew your passions daily.
TERRI GUILLEMETS

One person with passion is better than forty people merely interested."
E. M. FORSTER

I can't imagine a person becoming a success who doesn't give this game of life everything he's got."
WALTER CRONKITE

> There can not be a leader who does not have a passion. It is what may also be called a JUNOON.

48

The Critical Mass for a Tornado

Leadership does not act in vacuum. It is a people centric activity. But how many persons should follow someone for him to be termed a leader? The answer can vary depending on the situation at hand or the type of organisation. There is no hard and fast rule except that there got to be a certain critical mass of followers to an idea or a mission to make that vision gather momentum. This minimal strength is the critical mass or the threshold for quantum growth. Below it you may have ripples in the sea but to really make it a crescendo or a tornado the critical mass has to be present. Once it is there the energy generated by it can really do wonder. The energy released would be phenomenal. **Thus a leader should ensure that he constantly works towards building the critical mass of the desired purity (integrity, honesty and commitment) so that when it is charged for action, it shows results.**

A change management programme succeeds only when the change in processes and outcomes becomes embedded in the day to day working of the organisation. To make it work the critical mass of employees and mangers must be passionately involved in bringing the changes in outcome and processes.

The Critical Mass for a Tornado

When an idea reaches critical mass there is no stopping the shift its presence will induce.

MARIANNE WILLIAMSON

Take it to the max, Critical Mass!

GOTHAMIST

Thus a leader should ensure that he constantly works towards building the critical mass of the desired purity (integrity, honesty and commitment) so that when it is charged for action, it shows results.

49

Work – the Play Called Government

There is a saying that

"Give some one a job he loves and he will not have to work a single day".

We all might have heard the Leo Tolstoy story of 'white washing the fence; which conveys the same message. It is the pleasure of work that can do miracles. But can we make our jobs playful? The answer is an emphatic yes! It can be done. After all playing the game is.
1. An attitude.
2. Bound by well laid rules.
3. Some competition to get your goals – that keeps your adrenalin levels.
4. Internally driven.
5. You don't get bored by more play.

The same holds true for work. Once we start loving our work, its no longer stressful, rather its fun meeting endless stream of persons hour after hour and enjoying the journey called work. When people take their jobs as a play in serious sense they get directed into it with their mind, body and soul.

One can see how a soccer player wades through obstacle of 10 players for ninety minutes giving every bit of his energy and yet remain all cheerful. Government is also a game that begins with love all, and may end with a score of Love-All or 10-10 or 5-0. In cricket at a more intimate level we have all seen Sachin Tendulkar scoring century after century so effortlessly or our

grand old man Fauja Singh running marathon in UK at the age of 92 years and winning it. The thought itself of a man of 92 years running every day several kilometers and winning marathon is unbelievable, isn't it? But is has happened and it will happen again, we got to put the game mind set into our jobs or the task.

Here comes the role of a leader. He may be the captain of the team who has to constantly ensure the appropriate mix of enthusiasm into the game of governance. It would keep them charged endlessly and when discharged, recharged again with renewed energies.

> We all might have heard the Leo Tolstoy story of 'white washing the fence; which conveys the same message. It is the pleasure of work that can do miracles. But can we make all our jobs playful? The answer is an emphatic yes! It can be done.

50

The Upward Helix: It's a Continuous Growth Route

Organisations can choose the option of continuous growth, meaning that it grows both vertically as well as horizontally along the route. This is what pictorially we can call the upwards growing Helix.

This helix has a narrow base but over time it not only broadens its diameter it also moves up the continuous path. **The upwards growing helix should be the conceptual model along which a leader should plan his organisational strategy. Here the vertical and the horizontal growth should be seen in wider perspective and government offices are an ideal example.** Due to inadequate push the organisations have a tendency to stagnate and with such stagnation the employees, who constitute the organisation, too stagnate. An organisation can be so designed that it keeps its work force on a constant growth route. When employees grow the organisation growth also follows, for ultimately it is the collective performance of these employees that makes the organisation. As leader or head of the organisation one need to see that the path remains obstacle free and they remain suitably charged to move up the spiral of growth and change of continuous improvement. Moving along the upward spiral requires us to learn, commit and move on increasingly higher planes. It is a process that is continuously repeated at different level along the upward path.

The Road Less Traveled;

When one creates an organisational vision one is entering into an arena which is not well defined. Setting new visions, new goals, new directions means that the leader has taken a calculated risk to make the job some what challenging. These are roads that have not been explored earlier. It is here that the qualities of a leader are put to test for he has to marshal his skills, talent and other tools to pave way and steer towards the goal. In government offices we often come across such situation, eg:

1. A new agriculture development programme is initiated using new variety of seeds and agricultural practices for the first time. The crop being tried for the first time, agricultural officers have poor information on how the crop will behave to various agricultural practices.
2. Using a new vaccine to prevent some diseases or changing over from tablet to vaccine. Such changeover though done after extensive research trials, there are still several unexplained situation that can create complication due to genetic structures of different races, due to pre existing diseases or interferences with other drugs etc.
3. Switching over to new system of teaching in schools where the books and the teaching methodology have been changed after being successfully implemented in some other states. The behavior of teacher/students

being a complex interaction, such efforts have to be constantly tracked for sometime.

These situations polish the leadership and strengthen the team. It also gives confidence among the team managers of successfully handling a situation.

> The upwards growing helix should be the conceptual model along which a leader should plan his organisational strategy. Here the vertical and the horizontal growth should be seen in wider perspective and government offices are an ideal example.

51

Governments are Unique

The business of governance, like all businesses, is not an easy game. When we are looking for success in the job we are in, we need to take care of the innumerable unique features which our government system has. Government functioning is unique in several ways, such as ;

1. **Gigantic in size** – Indian Army, Indian Railways are two typical examples which employ more than 3 million persons on their pay roll.
2. **Different control system** – The control systems in public services are much different from the corporate world.
3. **The geographical dispersal of locations** – Almost all departments of government are spread over vast distances into villages, districts and small cities. We can find a Primary Health Care centre, an ICDS office, a village land record officer, or a village agriculture extension officer delivering various services in our villages across the country.
4. **Government is largely into services sector** – Railways, Health, Education, Airline, Banking, Sanitation, Water Supply, Power supply etc. are some illustrations. On the contrary corporate or private sector is largely into

manufacturing of goods and production processes like car manufacturing, production of machines, engineering goods, construction industry etc.
5. **Insurgency problems** – Government offices apart from having the problems of terrain like Hills, Rivers, Jungles, and Deserts have to sometime encounter problem like insurgency and terrorism also. Typical problem states are North-East, J&K. Chattisgarh, Jharkhand and Andhra Pradesh.

This uniqueness needs that the human resource deployed at these places are selected with care. One may have to take into consideration the nativeness, the language, or the cultural background of the person when selecting for a particular location, so that he is responsive towards their specific needs due to his comfort level on local culture.

In government one does not have a choice of choosing the place. There are services which have to be provided no matter what the cost may be. A typical example is the setting up of booths for voters during elections. There are several places where the election commission sets up booths only for a few persons for example in Kashmir, Laddakh and Arunachal. The setting up of these booths, the manpower and other logistics costs a huge amount. No wonder we are one of the most vibrant and dynamic democracies in the world.

All the above mentioned illustrations of gigantic size organisations need some strong systems in place so that the programmes do not go hay way. Some of these can be –

1. **Stay connected** – We are living in the I.T. era. With diverse tools like telephone, internet, mobile phone, fax and other electronic facilities available, it is very easy to keep track of various programmes and projects under implementation in the departments. These tools are

not luxuries but essentialities of any sturdy organization or office set up. It helps in keeping the organization employees updated on the latest and they do not falter on something vital. It is also a very useful coordination tool.

2. **Maintain consistency** – Consistency of approach in resolving issues of governance is very crucial. Well laid written instructions and procedures in black and white can achieve it.

3. **Problem Solving** – Physically dispersed offices employing thousands of personnel need quick redressal on employees' issues at local level. If these are not attended in time it leads to multiplicity of complex problems at a later date. One way of regular redressal is to hold monthly/fortnightly interaction of office heads with his team, other sub-ordinates and redress the problems that have cropped up due to a new government order, policy, and court order or for some other reasons. Video conferencing is a very useful tool which can help the department Heads, Chairman/Secretaries etc to speak directly to the field functionaries.

The dispersed presence in villages all over the country is a unique feature of our vibrant bureaucratic system. Using effectively and creatively this asset can be converted into the messenger of responsive administration, conveying that the government is always by their side to address to every emergency or problem that the citizen faces.

> In government one does not have a choice of choosing the place. There are services which have to be provided no matter what the cost may be. A typical example is the setting up of booths for voters during elections. There are several places where the election commission sets up booths only for a few persons for example in Kashmir, Laddakh and Arunachal.

52

Governance and Government

The past three decades have seen a resurgence of the issue of good governance. Though the phenomenon is observed worldwide, the developing countries like India got a special boost with their successive Prime Ministers putting governance as a focus area in their list of priorities. Good governance has today become a part of the evaluating criteria of international bodies like World Bank, IMF etc. This move has brought out some far reaching changes like deregulation, privatisation of certain sectors, liberalization etc. India, the largest democracy, has also downsized as part of good governance.

The initial four decades of post independent India had a strong socialistic component which saw the emergence of giant public sector units like, BHEL, HAL, HMT, Bokaro and Bhilai steel plants, fertilizer plants, shipyards etc. These and several other nation specific innovations have resulted that since 1990's we have been one of the fastest growing economies in the world. The challenge before us is now to move to double digit growth rate to be in the group of China, Korea, Singapore etc. India is today at this crucial juncture to jump to the group of top few. Improved public governance would take us to that stage.

A study of governance by World Bank has identified six dimension of governance; political instability, citizen participation, accountability, effectiveness, rule of law, and corruption. India has a mixed score on these chosen dimensions. The voice of rural areas being not adequately heard inefficient delivery system and bloated machinery, delays in decisions in almost all government processes etc are some issues that emerge out of it. The bureaucratic form of government which once facilitated management now tends to restrict innovations. The role of government in 21st Century seems to be more desired to be catalytic, community empowering, mission driven, competitive, result oriented and customer driven.

Governance has been defined as "the process of sharing power and authority, mediating interests and differences, and exercising rights and obligations among the three main stakeholders, including the government, private sector and citizens." It is only through the existence of a "governance relationship" that this transformation of the government can occur. The focus on "creating a conducive environment for growth and development and improving the efficiency of resource use, particularly in public sector, "finds place in the 10th five year plan document. It also outlines the issues and strategies: public participation, decentralisation, right to information, reform of the revenue system, civil service reforms, judicial reform, and use of I.T. etc for good governance.

Achieving good governance is a complex and multidisciplinary activity. The above mentioned characteristics of governance are complementary to one another and the satisfaction of any one component raises the probability that another will be satisfied and or its effects on development will be raised. Good governance and its operationalisation rest on process, values and institutions. The degree to which a given country's governance characteristics can be changed depends on its institutions and to that extent these are very important.

> Governance has been defined as "the process of sharing power and authority, mediating interests and differences, and exercising rights and obligations among the three main stakeholders, including the government, private sector and citizens." It is only through the existence of a "governance relationship" that this transformation of the government can occur.

53

Use of I.T. – Government @ the Speed of Light

If one thing that is growing at the fastest pace in India, it is the mobile phone users. A decade ago we were nowhere but today we have more than 40 crores mobile users in the country and have already become the fastest growing mobile user nation. This in itself is a landmark moment, for the mobile phone is not merely a phone its multiple feature and additionalties have made it one of the essentiality of a common man. A mobile phone is something like a mobile personal computer. One can make and receive call, send receive e-mail, use SMS, use as a camera, video camera, radio, TV and what not. All this has been possible due to revolution in the information technology. E-mails have today become routine in government transaction and the traffic using internet is not only getting speedier its volume is also growing rapidly. Our personal computers today provide work at the speed of light or at the speed of thought.

Internet, mobile and other similar technologies provide us the opportunity to always stay connected and have access to information. It also offers instantaneous results in the internet connected world. Whether taking an air ticket, drawing funds from bank, paying bill, planning vacation, ordering a book or buying anything else anywhere in the would has today become a reality. All this without the problem of delays, or bureaucratic apathy.

Use of I.T. has several district advantages over the traditional mode of government such as;

1. The services are prompt and hassle free
2. The authenticity of records is accepted
3. The capacity to store information is enormous
4. The option of simultaneous multiple facility access is a unique feature
5. Its global in nature
6. It can intelligently organise enormous data in a second
7. Every walk of work can use it.

Practically, the dealing with bureaucratic organisations is complicated but the transformation to this mode has really shown the way. We can see it working in

- E-Banking
- E-ticket (Airway and Railways)
- E-cards (virtually for everything now)
- E-passport
- Telemedicine
- E-Stocks (d-mat account)
- E-library etc.

It is observed that computerization of services in public sector is still a slow process and common citizen has to waste time and money to get small jobs done. Private sector has made rapid strides in almost all sectors but governments are still slow in this area. Some of the activities which each department or office can plan are –

a. Create a web portal for the office
b. Design a short 3-4 days course for every employee of the office on use of computers and associated tools.
c. Encourage transmission of information between various offices through internet.
d. Create web based data bank which could be utilized by all employees. It can display Acts, Rules and regulation, yearly progress reports on various programmes or other similar informations.
e. Encourage meetings and discussions using power point presentations.
f. Create citizen interactive web site on various department specific subjects.
g. Think about use of I.T. in day to day office work and public dealing such as smart cards (like Bank credit cards)

Use of information technology breaks the conventional communication and hierarchical barriers that exist in the bureaucratic setups. The new age of global village seeks for models that are flexible and compatible to the information driven economy. I.T. has that capacity to empower citizens apart from cutting the bureaucratic processes in delivering public services.

Electronic government will mean dramatic improvement in services (like e-ticket) and will redefine the relationship of government to citizen. It can enable the citizens to have greater access to more convenient, responsive and less expensive government services. It means speedier flow of information enabling better analysis and better decisions.

Use of information technology breaks the conventional communication and hierarchical barriers that exist in the bureaucratic setups. The new age of global village seeks for models that are flexible and compatible to the information driven economy.

54

Growth Continuum-Growing Up With the Organisation

Government is not only just about providing services and getting paid for it, it is something much more. It is an opportunity for the employee and the employer to grow along the path. The government is therefore a system which grows as it serves. This is what may be called the Growth Continuum. However, we may see that it doesn't actually happen in all cases. To make it happen in all organisations in government a leader is needed. Here the leader by appropriate mix of priorities, goals and strategies can transform the organisation to, growing up with the organisation mode. It is a win-win situation for the individual employee and the overall system called government. Growing with the organisation implies that;

1. The individuals are motivated and are performing their assigned duties in a mission mode with passion, and dedication.
2. The gains of government are suitably shared with the employees by way of awards to put them on a higher pedestal of performance for the next round of process.
3. The organisation over the years grows in terms of magnitude and also quality of its services.

This is a leader driven strategy that has to marshal all resources at his command and take the system to a higher level. Where the offices or the bureaucratic governmental organisations are left to themselves, it would drift at the mercy of winds and lead to nowhere. Such an unguided institution over time would decline in teams of output services, quality and everything that is associated with the issues of good governance.

An Organisation led by a well designed strategy and driven by a leadership committed to a vision would move constantly upwards.

All organisations should ideally dream for a growth path that could be described in an upward growing helix. Such an organisation, its employees and other stakeholders would always be part of a win-win scenario.

55

Keep the Team Motivated

Motivation can be defined as the skill of energising yourself and others to accomplish something positive. To be a leader you need to be a motivator of your people and also yourself. As a leader you need to make other people feel better by making him more motivated. You also need to ensure that he continues this link with other persons who come in his contact. Motivation keeps the persons energised so that he is on his targets with greater enthusiasm and vigour. Apart from motivating others a leader has to see that he himself is also motivated.

The Process of motivating yourself or someone else involves several stages which lead to a motivated person. First comes developing a vision of success. This vision should be backed by faith & confidence. In such an environment the positive feedback uplifts the confidence and boosts up the motivation process. The motivational path is guided by the vision of success. This vision need to be backed by a brief workable action plan and should not be something vague. As leader of the team or head of office you need to present this roadmap to success with enthusiasm so that it infuses & energises the team and gives them confidence. Dealing with large workforce in governments it is essential to keep the programmes in good pace or keep the team woven around some common driver. These can be some sort of incentives like money, power, accomplishment, respect, recognition, rewards etc.

> The Process of motivating yourself or someone else involves several stages which lead to a motivated person. First comes developing a vision of success. This vision should be backed by faith & confidence. In such an environment the positive feedback uplifts the confidence and boosts up the motivation process.

56

Competence – Let it Grow All Around

Leadership is not about some vague of nebulous entity. It is about leading the team of fellow colleagues and subordinates. Leadership in governmenl or bureaucratic systems also means that the workforce is professional. Competency in administration not only means focused work, it also means that the persons performing it are more focused and clear about what they are dealing with and why a certain course of action is better. Competency among employees has a positive effect on the organisation as a whole, particularly the human resource which is the core of any organisation. For any profession or work place it means whether a person can undertake what is required to be done by him at the desired levels of performance. In a professional scenario it means –

1. That the person has certain desirable technical or professional qualifications which are a precondition for him to be on that job. It usually means the academic qualification.
2. That he has received some professional or work related trainings that make him a more informed or

knowledgeable person in respect of others. It may mean having a training in accounting or budget, financial analysis, or project approvals, or other job specific skill like specialization in handling boiler problems, aircraft air conditioning etc.
3. The person uses those skills in his work place on a day to day basis on issues that are posed to him.

In administrative works it means;

- The person is updated on various laws and regulations that govern his works (such as health manual, works manual etc.)
- The person is updated on various guidelines, protocols and instructions issued related to work performance and he uses them at certain desired level of acceptance.

These are to be used by competent professional in routine manner. If one is an engineer, the reference to various manuals indicates that he is aware about the technicalities relating to that work. Similarly a professional approach to a problem would mean studying it from the legal, regulatory and other contexts. It is observed that there is an approach among bureaucracy to deal work in a general manner rather than analysing and arriving on conclusion based on laws, regulations, manuals, guidelines or documented precedence. Professional competence is to been seen in the work done by an individual. His seal of in depth understanding of the issues should speak out from the way he deals with the problems.

Professional competence is a continuous process which should grow on the individual and should be widely promoted among the employees. It makes the employees approach problem in a systematic and methodical way

which have been extensively tested and verified like a professional protocol for an open heart surgery or dealing with trauma cases.

Another aspect of professionalism is the competence of interpersonal relationship. All problems or issues have a human aspect too. Ultimately we are dealing with human beings who are working on any issue. These inter personal skills can also be developed and acquired by professional training programmes. Labour or management issues at time get stuck on issues which require competence of a different nature – The competence of man management. Professional trainings if taken earlier come very handy.

In bureaucratic organisations we regularly come across what is commonly referred as administrative competence which is the above approach applied to administrative tasks. Administrative or professional competence is an asset that can be grown constantly by each individual. He can constantly update himself by doing new professional or academic courses which can enrich him professionally and academically apart from giving him an edge over other persons.

> Professional competence is a continuous process which should grow on the individual and should be widely promoted among the employees. It makes the employees approach problem in a systematic and methodical way which have been extensively tested and verified like a professional protocol for an open heart surgery or dealing with trauma cases.

57

Take Responsibility for Action

In Government quite often we come across a situation where one has to identity the person who has brought the organisation some fame. One would never find problem in identifying such leader for there would be several persons claiming credit for such positive transformations. However, when certain developments, lead to some problems one would find that there would be none ready to take responsibility. A typical example can be a train derailment or some other accident or a police firing that leads to death of some person. One will notice that it would be a very difficult process in government to exactly pin point the person responsible for the mishap. True leadership, lies in owning up responsibility for ones actions good or bad. On several occasions we have situation where a certain decision did not yield the expected results. This does not mean that you hang the person who took that decision. The owning up of responsibility is a trait of growing leadership. Leaders should see that where a decision is not mala fide or rash, they should evaluate how the organisation can learn from that experience. There are certain individuals who would like to corner all the glory but would find a scape goat if there is failure. Such actions should be avoided.

Accountability is more significant for those who also have the authority as it is authority that gives, an individual to make thing happen in a certain way.

"I must do something" always solves more problems than "Something must be done."
AUTHOR UNKNOWN

The willingness to accept responsibility for one's own life is the source from which self-respect springs.
JOAN DIDION

Most of us can read the writing on the wall; we just assume it's addressed to someone else.
IVERN BALL

We need to restore the full meaning of that old word, duty. It is the other side of rights.
PEARL BUCK

I believe that every right implies a responsibility; every opportunity, an obligation; every possession, a duty.
JOHN D. ROCKEFELLER, JR.

Take your life in your own hands, and what happens? A terrible thing: no one to blame.
ERICA JONG

The best years of your life are the ones in which you decide your problems are your own. You do not blame them on your mother, the ecology, or the president. You realize that you control your own destiny.
ALBERT ELLIS

A new position of responsibility will usually show a man to be a far stronger creature than was supposed.
WILLIAM JAMES

God has entrusted me with myself.
EPICTETUS

We are made wise not by the recollection of our past, but by the responsibility for our future.

GEORGE BERNARD SHAW

True leadership, lies in owning up responsibility for ones actions good or bad. On several occasions we have situation where a certain decision did not yield the expected results. This does not mean that you hang the person who took that decision. The owning up of responsibility is a trait of growing leadership.

58

Bureaucratic Accountability

Governance is the key issue for any ruling party. It means transforming the broad policy directives into implementable action points. This is the stage where the administrative competence of government comes into play. No matter how best the political action plans be, the onus for the last mile connectivity lies with the administrators. **The Civil servant is the critical link in the continuum of governance. In that capacity the bureaucrat-civil servants are responsible for good implementation and with it also comes the question that the bureaucrat is accountable, he is answerable.**

Over the past decade or two on a large number of occasions it is being noticed that an issue which could be handled by a station house officer gets escalated to a level that it leads the intervention of the head of district. The reason for this is the abdication of responsibility. Even for petty law & order issues one starts looking up to the political system for guidance or advise. In this process the simple issues get complicated and in case it leads to a failure, the responsibility is passed on to the political system. The Kargil war or several other large scale law & order problems can be traced back to some dereliction of duty by some bureaucrat at some stage. More often than not it is seen that effective responsibility is not fixed on those who are at the helm of affairs.

Administration is not one isolated activity, It is the assimilation of several interconnected issues which ultimately produces results. The collapse of a bridge over a river or the head on collision of two trains, An aeroplane hitting a stray cattle on the runway or a person dying in police custody are all examples where accountability can be fixed and should be fixed so that in the ultimate analysis the governance in the net gainer. Effective governance is a continuum of responsibility both for the politician & the civil servant and it is the differentiation of the roles that would make the governments function more effectively in a more accountable manner.

At the cutting edge of administration it is essential that bureaucrats realise their responsibility and act with clarity as they are going to be the gainer.

> The Civil servant is the critical link in the continuum of governance. In that capacity the bureaucrat-civil servants are responsible for good implementation and with it also comes the question that the bureaucrat is accountable, he is answerable.

59

Declutter the Work Place

One typical sight we come across public, offices and workplaces is cluttering of the place. There is lot of Junk around. A Cluttered, place apart from eating into the precious office space also conveys a very poor perception in the mind of common citizen who visit our offices for various services. It does not look aesthetically appropriate. Broken furniture, heap of files, files stacked un systematically, lot of useless out dated things dumped over the place etc.

A clean work place silently speaks about the clean work environment. It creates positive vibes among the staff working in such work place. It is easier to organise the work in a more spacious and aesthetically planned work place. Weeding out papers, old files, furniture and other junk material should be a regular activity among all offices. Do it and feel the de stressed expression on every face.

A Cleaned up office also generates orderliness. It means it is easier to locate a file among the stack of papers in your office. Decluttering is an exercise in organising our self and our work place. Some tips can be:

    a.   Keep only the project you are currently handling on your table.

Declutter the Work Place 171

b. Files and papers which have come during the day can be kept in the 'in' files shelf so that you always know how much work needs your attention.
c. Have proper filing system
d. Don't have your desk face the exit
e. Keep only 3 to 4 chairs in your room. Excess chairs encourage people to sit down.
f. Discourage barge in visitors. They are a big time wasters

A clean work place silently speaks about the clean work environment. It creates positive vibes among the staff working in such work place. It is easier to organise the work in a more spacious and aesthetically planned work place.

60

Work Called Play

There is a saying

> *The true way to render ourselves happy is to love our work and find in it our pleasure.*

The saying nicely captures the relationship between job and work. In fact all leaders and head of offices should create environment where people enjoy the work they do. In real life situation it is a very difficult proposition but we can create situation in our organisation that makes the job some thing to feel happy about. Some ways to achieve this are:

a. Make them more aware about their job and its significance in the totality of things.
b. Train them so that they become more competent to do their Jobs in a better manner.
c. Allocating work to individuals according to their capability.
d. Constantly nurture staff so that they get empowered to perform better.
e. Appreciating them whenever they do a good job. Repeated appreciation develops in them, the love for their work,

f. Giving rewards or other incentives as they achieve some landmark.

When we bring the change in our staff from work to play we will notice that work does not remain drudgery to them and it helps them reach their performance levels quickly. Such an environment would also facilitate creativity in the organisation.

Opportunity is missed by most because it is dressed in overalls and looks like work.

THOMAS ALVA EDISON

Happiness, it seems to me, consists of two things: first, in being where you belong, and second -- and best -- in comfortably going through everyday life, that is, having had a good night's sleep and not being hurt by new shoes.

THEODOR FONTANE

I don't wait for moods. You accomplish nothing if you do that. Your mind must know it has got to get down to work. Pearl S. Buck

People rarely succeed unless they have fun in what they are doing.

DALE CARNEGIE

The secret of joy in work is contained in one word – excellence. To know how to do something well is to enjoy it.

PEARL S. BUCK.

People might not get all they work for in this world, but they must certainly work for all they get.

FREDERICK DOUGLASS

The true way to render ourselves happy is to love our work and find in it our pleasure.

FRANCOISE DE MOTTEVILLE

Dreams pass into the reality of action. From the actions stems the dream again; and this interdependence produces the highest form of living.

ANAIS NIN

61

Tatkal Sewa

Some years ago Indian Railways introduced a train reservation facility called Tatkal Sewa. This facility provided an opportunity of fast reservation at an extra cost to last minute passengers. The scheme is today providing good services to millions of passengers in addition to generating additional revenues for the railways.

When mobile and internet have reduced time in communicating between two ends to zero Tatkal or Prompt Service is today the need of our times. Whether it is an E-Sewa or some other internet based innovation, the concept behind all should be prompt attention to customers and disposal of the work for which he has come to that office. In government offices it is essential that every individual identifies how he can add his bit to the promptness in services. Some interventions which all offices can do are;

1. Listening patiently to the individual grievances
2. Make a phone call to expedite his matter
3. Write a letter to the agency at whose level the matter is pending and give this open letter to the visitor. It would have a salutary effect. Do all that is needed to expeditiously do the task.

Remember-Speed is the need of our times.

62

Meetings and Minutes

Governments move on papers and every action or reaction of any government official has to be supported by a properly drafted proceeding. Meetings of various type are an essential part of every bureaucrat's life. There are various types of meeting that are taken by ministers or senior officials. These are very important meetings that deal with a lot of policy or important programme issues. Therefore it is essential that;

1. The decisions get properly recorded
2. The decisions are promptly approved
3. It gets quickly conveyed to the concerned officials for action.

It has been observed that on a large number of occasions the minutes are not properly recorded, or are recorded by a junior official, it takes time to draft and long time to get conveyed to the end users. These issues can be effectively addressed if the chairman of such meetings records the minutes in the meeting itself and by the time the meeting finish the minutes are also final and can be sent by e mail or by hand. Such continuous minutisation of the decisions has the following advantages;

a. The minutes are dictated by the chair and recorded on computer leaving little scope for ambiguity.
b. As the minutes are recorded in the meeting the participants can also point out any other relevant aspect that needs to be recorded.
c. It shows urgency and seriousness of the issues.
d. The emphasis at relevant places can be highlighted.
e. By the time the meeting finishes the minutes are ready.
f. It can be circulated in the meeting or later sent by an e-mail.

Time is the essence and this approach greatly helps in making the decisions reach the end users immediately. I have personally applied it for more than a decade and seen that it works wonderfully well.

> It has been observed that on a large number of occasions the minutes are not properly recorded, or are recorded by a junior official, it takes time to draft and long time to get conveyed to the end users. These issues can be effectively addressed if the chairman of such meetings records the minutes in the meeting itself and by the time the meeting finish the minutes are also final and can be sent by e mail or by hand.

63

Jump the Levels

The big problem with bureaucracy is the multiplicity of levels both horizontal as well as vertical. This not only complicates the organizational dynamics in terms of dealing with an issue at hand, it also means delay in arriving at a decision. In government it has been observed that the traditional methods of staff empowerment, development of systems, training and skill development take a lot of time. Even if government provides such training there is no guaranteeing that the person would be assigned the job for which he is most suitable.

How to cut short the time taken in arriving at critical decisions? Various methods have been adopted to cut the red tape and the delays in making decision. One method that really works well in large organisations like government is level jumping. In plain term it means reducing the number of persons handling a matter for decision. Take an example of Health Department where we have multiple levels of Principal Secretary, Secretary, Commissioner, Director, Joint Director, Chief Medical Officer, and Block Medical Officer.

1. Principal Secretary
2. Secretary

3. Commissioner
4. Director
5. Joint Director
6. Chief Medical Officer
7. Block Medical Officer

In the above scenerio the bottom two are the field functionaries who deal with the programmes at block level and the others are the ones dealing with policy issues. Thus decisions have to move up from level 7 to 1 through the mesh of the multilevel hierarchy and there is no surety that it would reach the ultimate level. It may get scuttled at any level in between.

For major projects or programmes that are scaled up over large areas it is essential that the levels are kept to the minimum, say 2 to 3. This can be done by doing away with the intermediate ones. I have seen that

1. It works better
2. Promotes innovation
3. It motivates the team to action and produce excellent results.

Level jumping is a leadership activity and it is for the heads to decide who can jump what levels. In develops confidence among team mates apart from speedy flow of papers.

> How to cut short the time taken in arriving at critical decisions? Various methods have been adopted to cut the red tape and the delays in making decision. One method that really works well in large organisations like government is level jumping. In plain term it means reducing the number of persons handling a matter for decision.

64

Seeing is Believing and Eye Opening Too

As one moves up the hierarchical ladder in government one gets more and more detached from the ground reality of his organization. The day to day work pressure and other routine matters leave little time with organizational heads to see what all is actually happening within the institution and its offices.

All the organizational heads and leaders should stay in constant touch with the core activities at the cutting edge level. One need not go a hundred kilometer to see it, the village next to the office or the locality across the road can throw ample light on how the core programmes are going on. Such visits/inspections or interactions with the citizens and staff would also provoke newer approaches to address a challenge on hand. It would give an excellent feedback from the citizens without the comments of the middle level officials. Such visits should be done as frequently as possible and may touch upon different aspects of work; one may share the organizational dream or interact with them to understand the work better. Power, Telecommunication, Postal, Water Supply, Revenue, Housing, Public Health etc are some such citizen centric departments that can extensively use it. In fact it is useful to all wings of government. Some of the things one can look into are;

Ask Questions

It is a great opportunity to observe those "moments of truth" when your employees interact with your clients. Ask them to tell you a little bit about the projects they are working on.

Watch and Listen

Take in everything. Listen to the words and tone of employees as they speak to you and to each other. You'll learn a lot about their motivation and their levels of satisfaction. You can observe a lot just by watching.

Share Your Dreams with Them

Tell them about the organization's vision for the future, and where your vision for the department /unit/section fits in with the "big picture." Reveal the goals and objectives that you want them to help you fulfill together as a team. Ask them for their vision, and hold an open discussion.

Try Out Their Work

Sit down in front of the computer; pick up the telephone; review a project file. Sample their job just enough to show your interest in it, and to understand how it goes. Think of great ways to reconnect with your field staff, and get understanding of exactly what they are dealing with during a typical work day.

Bring Good News

Walk around armed with information about recent successes or positive initiatives. Give them the good news. Increase their confidence and brighten their outlook. So often employees are fed only gloom and doom, neutralize pessimism with your own optimism.

Have Fun

This is a chance to lighten up, joke around, and show your softer side without being disrespectful. Show employees that work should be fun and that you enjoy it too.

Catch Them in the Act of Doing Something Right

Look for victories rather than failures. When you find one, applaud it. When you run into one of the many unsung heroes in your job site, thank them on the spot, being careful not to leave out other deserving employees.

Don't Be Critical

When you witness a performance gone wrong, don't criticize the performer. Correct on the spot anything that must be redone.

Keep the Team in Full Strength

One typical problem in all large departments in government is the large number of vacant posts at various levels. This problem becomes serious as without proper manpower in place one can not perform at its best. It is all the more significant as employment in government is an area of priority.

Human resource management at all levels is a critical activity that leaders need to periodically look into. It can reveal

1. The status of vacancies in the set up.
2. The progress of filling them up.
3. The bottlenecks in filling up such posts.

This is a win-win game. By filling up these posts we strengthen our organization which in turn would help in deliver better. Regular promotions also send a positive signal to the team.

> All the organizational heads and leaders should stay in constant touch with the core activities at the cutting edge level. One need not go a hundred kilometer to see it, the village next to the office or the locality across the road can throw ample light on how the core programmes are going on.

65

Daily Continuous Learning

Bureaucrats world over have a tendency to stagnate as far as the learning for new things is concerned. Once an officer or a civil servant enters the job with certain skills invariably he retires with the same skills. In the rapidly changing national scenario it is essential that all of us keep ourself abreast by acquiring new thoughts and tool that would make us professionally more competent. Our professional knowledge learned through academic courses or otherwise facilitates in putting us in that mode.

We should not rest on our past achievements but make a habit to think daily about making our work better. This could mean bringing about various changes. It may also mean mid course correction on some existing programme and setting new agendas.

66

Stay Ahead

A leader has the responsibility to always think ahead of others only then he can manage to retain his position. Staying at top would mean that the entire team of officials and subordinates are adequately geared up as it is the synergised action of the organisation as a whole which would keep you in lead.

In government it may means keeping track of performance of various programme at the national level and evaluate where we stand and what changes are needed to pace up to catch up with others. In government set up we have to compete with ourselves.

Staying ahead would require that the employees are motivated to internalize change and it occupies high priority on the agenda.

67

Work Hard – Party Hard

Government employees are known to work hard for long hours. Such work also leads to states achieving outstanding performance or the department, a particular office achieving distinction or an award in a particular area. It is seen that such achievement both at the orgnisation and at the individual level go un noticed or celebrated among the employees, who in their own way have contributed to the success. **We do not celebrate and it is considered a taboo in bureaucracy. By celebrating success regularly with the team we can develop a culture that promotes camaraderie.** Our team knows that if they are cheering for Mr Aditya tomorrow it could be their turn too.

Such celebrations apart from providing a relaxed environment to staff to open up and enjoy the journey to success also makes them create a dream to another bigger celebration.

> We do not celebrate and it is considered a taboo in bureaucracy. By celebrating success regularly with the team we can develop a culture that promotes camaraderie.

68

Fun at Workplace

"People rarely succeed unless they have fun in what they are doing."

Dale Carnegie

As a leader of your team and organization, it is your responsibility to create and nurture a positive work environment for your employees. Adding a little fun to the workplace does not have to be a major ordeal. In fact, by using some very simple techniques and tools, you can create positive energy while also gaining ground on your work objectives.

Creating friendly competition among peer groups is a great way to spice up the day. The rewards do not have to be expensive. In fact, sometimes the best reward doesn't cost any more than a little time and effort. You may even be surprised how seriously your team members will take the challenge. Even if there are no actual prizes involved, your team will want to win "bragging rights" over their peers.

In the story "White washing a Fence" by L. Tolstoy the key moral of the story was that, it is our attitude which makes an activity work for A but the same activity is play for B. It is the attitude and the objective with which we do the job which holds the key to work and fun. There is a saying

> "Give some one a Job he loves and he will not have to work a single day".

We all know that play is always de stressing and exhilarating, it makes us feel better. It can be seen that if you declare in the mid of a day at 1 pm that the days work is closing at 1.30 pm. the message spreads like wild fire and people make beeline to the exit gate & the office is deserted by 2 pm.

Work consists of whatever a body is obliged to do. Play consists of whatever a body is not obliged to do.
MARK TWAIN

Nobody can be successful unless he loves his work."
DAVID SARNOFF

"Live and work but do not forget to play, to have fun in life and really enjoy it."
EILEEN CADDY

69

Prevent the Cost Over Run

Cost and time over run is a typical problem in infrastructure projects in government and the delay is not in months but goes into years. This apart from burden on the exchequer also makes the citizens suffer various hardships due to lack of infrastructure. It is noticed in almost all the departments that they are not able to utilise the budget allocated to them for a particular year or for a particular project within the stipulated time. Preventing the cost over run is an issue that is related to systemic changes in the way department function.

Preventing the cost & time overrun is a leadership issue, departments can achieve it by

    a. **Making people accountable:** It is seen that various district and subordinate officials in sub division or Block level do not feel the responsibility that has been entrusted to them through that project. Executing any infrastructure or construction project, no matter how small it may be, needs coordination among various players for lands, material, budget, sanctions etc. and this calls for sense of responsibility & accountability. The message down the line should be that you suffer if you do not perform, if you do not deliver.

b. **Funds are a non-issue:** I have seen that funds are never a serious issue. On the contrary it is the other way round; Smart departments draw on the failure of other and get bonus allocation for performing better. Since budget is available a well-implemented project can be speeded up & completed before time.
c. **Monitor:** Weekly, fortnightly or monthly monitoring of how the budget is being spent can give a very clear picture of the affairs of the department. As leader & heads we should address them immediately & provide guidance whenever needed.

Budget is a very-very vital tool in monitoring and it helps in giving direction to the organisation.

70

Dress for Success

There is a saying; "Dressed to Kill". It is definitely an exaggeration but dresses do make an impression on people with whom you interact. **It is said that the first 15 seconds of your appearance at a meeting are most crucial as that is the time first opinion about you is formed on those present there.**

The appearances should therefore be paid attention to convey the right impression. Some ground rules on how to achieve the correct look are:

a. Keep to classic traditional colors like black, blue and grey for normal working suits.
b. The dress colors are coordinated with the environment around you. Shoes & Belts are paid attention.
c. Before stepping out for office give yourself a minute to check out how you look, your hairstyle, your shoes, the after shave or other such accessories.
d. Try to blend your dress with the culture of the place and with your own style. One can wear an Indian Achkan or a Jacket or traditional kurta to suit the occasion.
e. Always keep the body clean, fresh and smelling good. One can shave as many times as needed in the day.

Looking good is an effortless natural process that does not cost extra money but it definitely exudes energy, cheerfulness and a happy disposition, so vital for a successful person.

One is not fully dressed until one adorn oneself with a smile.

Clothes make the man.
LATIN PROVERB

Eat to please thyself, but dress to please others.
BENJAMIN FRANKLIN

"Dressing is a way of life."
YVES SAINT LAURENT

Language is the dress of thought.
SAMUEL JOHNSON

"I had no idea of the character. But the moment I was dressed, the clothes and the make-up made me feel the person he was. I began to know him, and by the time I walked onto the stage he was fully born.
CHARLIE CHAPLIN

Clothes don't make the man, but clothes have got many a man a good job.
HERBERT HAROLD VREELAND"

"I taught him how to dress. He taught me how to live forever."
LEONARD COHEN

"Who Dressed You Like a Foreigner?"
ZAKIR HUSSAIN

It is said that the first 15 seconds of your appearance at a meeting are most crucial as that is the time first opinion about you is formed on those present.

71

Give Result Not Excuses

Bureaucracy has the typical problem that if you have to pin point the responsibility for a catastrophe or a bad decision you may have to meander through a complex jungle of rules and procedure and yet the end may not be in sight. We are lost in the procedural complexity and not bothered about the end result. We should shift the focus from rules to results. Rules are meant to give results and not to act as road blocks, when they become road block its time to change them for something simpler, clearer and speedier version.

People have a tendency to cite rules as excuse for non-performance. Leaders should ensure that such persons are watched and suitably reoriented so that they are aligned with spirit of the objective at hand.

> *However beautiful the strategy, you should occasionally look at the results.*
>
> WINSTON CHURCHILL

> *There is no such thing as failure. There are only results.*
>
> TONY ROBBINS

> *Insanity: doing the same thing over and over again and expecting different results.*
>
> ALBERT EINSTEIN

If you want to be successful, find someone who has achieved the results you want and copy what they do and you'll achieve the same results.
                                                    TONY ROBBINS

I've always believed that if you put in the work, the results will come.
                                                    MICHAEL JORDAN

The achievements of an organization are the results of the combined effort of each individual.
                                                    VINCE LOMBARDI

If you tell people where to go, but not how to get there, you'll be amazed at the results.
                                                    GEORGE S. PATTON

Don't tell people how to do things, tell them what to do and let them surprise you with their results.
                                                    GEORGE S. PATTON

I worked hard. Anyone who works as hard as I did can achieve the same results.
                                                    JOHANNES SEBASTIAN BACH

The results you achieve will be in direct proportion to the effort you apply.
                                                    DENIS WAITLEY

Regardless of how you feel inside, always try to look like a winner. Even if you are behind, a sustained look of control and confidence can give you a mental edge that results in victory.
                                                    DIANE ARBUS

72

Unwanted Papers – Destroy them Immediately

Government offices get a large bulk of unwanted papers. These could be –

a. An unsolicited local magazine
b. Publicity material sent by some agency
c. Letters sent by companies seeking work with your organization.
d. Anonymous letters of complaints.
e. Annual reports of organization unconnected with your work.

Such papers should be destroyed at the first level itself i.e. the boss. They not only take time of the boss, it also eats into the time of the staff down the line. It would also save the need to store it or file it.

Apart from such obvious junk that goes into the offices, there is the other trivial correspondence of casual or short term nature, such as:–

- A complaint about air conditioner
- Acknowledgement of the joining report

- Arrangements for a VIP visit
- Other papers of minor significance.

All staff should periodically weed out such papers from their desks so that the focus remains in sight clearly and boldly.

73

Change – the Only Certainty At All Level

Every moment and everyday is new. Local and global changes while throwing new opportunities expose us to new threats also. Government employees have a tendency to stay status quoist- they resist change. But really speaking they are changing by inaction; they are relegated to lower position in the competitive world. All of us must have a mind set willing to embrace change. Change could be political, administrative, technical, attitudinal, social or any thing similar. In large organizations like governments things have not been attended for decades. Such inaction apart from making the system rot also makes it distanced from the reality around us.

Vibrant and dynamic institutions like government should continuously replenish itself with fresh thoughts. Millions of employees can collectively think and make organization a wonderful place. Every employee has certain ideas about what changes he wants in his work place. It may be within his capacity or may need support from seniors. Whatever an individual can change in his limits, he should do immediately and make efforts for others with assistance from seniors.

Indian bureaucracy is among the largest in the world. Thus the changes if coordinated and synergized can also lead to one of the largest change processes in the world. Such change processes where each employee is contributing his own bit can ultimately create a situation where positive changes that take the department to top position in the respective area can be seen and felt all along the organization. That is what a Leader in Government is meant to do. Such changes based on involvement of every employee are the need of our times.

If you don't like something change it; if you can't change it, change the way you think about it.
MARY ENGELBREIT

When you are through changing, you are through.
BRUCE BARTON

They must often change, who would be constant in happiness or wisdom.
CONFUCIUS

It is not the strongest of the species that survive, nor the most intelligent, but the one most responsive to change.
CHARLES DARWIN

Be the change you want to see in the world.
M K GANDHI

The wheel of change moves on, and those who were down go up and those who were up go down.
JAWAHARLAL NEHRU

Continuity gives us roots; change gives us branches, letting us stretch and grow and reach new heights.
PAULINE R. KEZER

God grant me the serenity to accept the people I cannot change, the courage to change the one I can, and the wisdom to know it's me.
AUTHOR UNKNOWN

The only man I know who behaves sensibly is my tailor; he takes my measurements anew each time he sees me. The rest go on with their old measurements and expect me to fit them.
> GEORGE BERNARD SHAW

If you change the way you look at things, the things you look at change.
> WAYNE DYER

If the facts don't fit the theory, change the facts.
> ALBERT EINSTEIN

Progress is impossible without change, and those who cannot change their minds cannot change anything.
> GEORGE BERNARD SHAW

Vibrant and dynamic institutions like government should continuously replenish itself with fresh thoughts. Millions of employees can collectively think and make organization a wonderful place. Every employee has certain ideas about what changes he wants in his work place. It may be within his capacity or may need support from seniors.

74

Love Your Self: Love Your Work

Our work is an extension of our personality, our core values and the wider vision that integrates us in the broad spectrum of government. You will find that persons who are not only well dressed, composed, prompt and clean in their office their attitude out side the working hours also reflects a similar person. When we love ourself our total attitude towards work change. Such as-

1. **Our dress** – We care about how we look, what we wear and its appropriateness to the occasion. We ensure that the clothes are neat, well maintained and match with our shoes, our hair are well kept & there may be a gentle fragrance.
2. **Our work place** – It would be tidy and orderly and there may be a flower pot adding beauty to the place.
3. **Disposition** – A happy and pleasant disposition in dealing with people.
4. **Speed** – Promptness in disposal of work.
5. **Worthiness** – Generally happy that one is putting one's time to fruitful use.

What we are visible to the outside world is what we are inside for we can pretend to be what we are not, but can not hide what we are.

It is therefore essential that we invest in ourself by loving ourselves and do things that make us internally strong, happy and satisfied. **Ultimately it is this that is going to be delivered to the outside world. When we love ourselves we also tend to normally start loving our Job, which is our bread and butter and which gives a purpose to our life.** Loving ourself is a conscious act and a very natural one for all of us because we all want to look great and want a reputation of a performer. Such a harmony apart from bringing happiness in whatever we do, also optimises our work.

> *Work is love made visible. And if you cannot work with love but only with distaste, it is better that you should leave your work and sit at the gate of the temple and take alms of those who work with joy.*
>
> KAHLIL GIBRAN

> *The Grand essentials of happiness are: something to do, something to love, and something to hope for.*
>
> ALLAN K. CHALMERS

> *If you have love in your life it can make up for a great many things you lack. If you don't have it, no matter what else there is... it's not enough.*
>
> ANN LANDERS

> *If you aren't good at loving yourself, you will have a difficult time loving anyone, since you'll resent the time and energy you give another person that you aren't even giving to yourself.*
>
> BARBARA DE ANGELIS

> *Who so loves, believes the impossible.*
>
> ELIZABETH BARRET BROWNING

> *If you cannot work with love but only with distaste, it is better that you should leave your work.*
>
> KAHLIL GIBRAN

Love and work... work and love, that's all there is.
SIGMUND FREUD

Don't sacrifice your life to work and ideals.
The most important things in life are human relations.
I found that out too late.
KATHARINDE SUSANNAH PRICHARD

It is not work that kills men; it is worry. Work is healthy; you can hardly put more upon a man than he can bear. Worry is rust upon the blade. It is not the revolution that destroys the machinery, but the friction. Fear secretes acids, but love and trust are sweet juices.
BEECHER

For one human being to love another that is perhaps the most difficult of our tasks; the ultimate, the last test and proof; the work for which all other work is but preparation.
RAINER MARIA RILKE

It is therefore essential that we invest in our self by loving ourselves and do things that make us internally strong, happy and satisfied. Ultimately it is this that is going to be delivered to the out side world. When we love ourselves we also tend to normal start loving our Job, which is our bread and butter and which gives a purpose to our life.

75

Small Steps – Keep Moving

Ask any head of department in government about the state of affairs and you will get a long list of reasons and problems that are pulling down the organisation or putting brakes on the pace of programmes or other campaigns. Frequent transfers, outdated rules, demotivated work force, poor skill & indiscipline etc. may be some of the grudges one may hear. It's likely that much of it may be trivial. **Notwithstanding such problems leaders in government have a responsibility to perform, to deliver and to bring about the desired change. Looking to the distance the organisation has to travel to catch up and pace up, the employees' team may get disheartened to go ahead and reach the destination if it is not regularly charged up.** As a strategy I have noticed that two things that helped and worked well are:

a: Take small steps: On any task at hand which has not been attended to for long like pending bank recoveries or removal of encroachment from government lands, it is advisable to make a small beginning for first quarter, say 20% of the year and target your energies on achieving this limited task. As one moves in achieving this small objective one regains the lost confidence. These small victories by the organisation or the department help in relearning the art of work and put the work on track in fast speed.

b. **Keep moving:** On several occasions some minor obstacles upset the entire movement which a programme or campaign has achieved. It is very essential for leaders that they should take charge of the situation on such occasion and through their leadership and administrative skill steer the organisation clear of the obstacles. The key to success is that such digression should not disturb us from our objective. The show must go on at a steady pace. These small successes be used as a fuel to the continued efforts.

Sometimes the cards we are dealt are not always fair. However you must keep smiling & moving on

Tom Jackson

Life is about making the right decisions and moving on.

Jos

You are responsible for your life. You can't keep blaming somebody else for your dysfunction. Life is really about moving on.

Oprah Winfrey

Courage is not the absence of fear, but simply moving on with dignity despite that fear.

Pat Riley

"Life is like riding a bicycle. To keep your balance you must keep moving.

Albert Einstein

The art of war is simple enough. Find out where your enemy is. Get at him as soon as you can. Strike him as hard as you can, and keep moving on.

Ulysses S. Grant

"Success seems to be connected with action. Successful people keep moving. They make mistakes, but they don't quit."

Conrad Hilton

"If you can dream it, you can do it. Always remember that this whole thing was started with a dream and a mouse."

WALT DISNEY

We keep moving forward, opening new doors, and doing new things, because we're curious and curiosity keeps leading us down new paths.

WALT DISNEY

If everyone is moving forward together, then success takes care of itself.

HENRY FORD

> Notwithstanding such problems leaders in government have a responsibility to perform, to deliver and to bring about the desired change. Looking to the distance the organisation has to travel to catch up and pace up, the employees' team may get disheartened to go ahead and reach the destination if it is not regularly charged up.

76

Continuous Search for Excellence Through Innovation

We are all in government to make things happen and produce results, the elements of management viz. planning, organizing, directing, motivating, coordination and controlling have the common aim to make things happens to achieve results. All leaders will have to see that they are "doing right things rather than doing things right". Leaders in government have to move out from the caretaker mode to the builder & to the creator mode. The better one does, the more he can go.

Governments are a vast mass of diverse and geographically dissociated departments dealing with thousands, of issues. As heads or leaders in government it is essential that creativity and innovation are activated at all levels. Devoid of this, management is simply a flat tube. It is innovation that activates and fires the whole process of management. If we look around any successful project or programme, at its core we will find result oriented innovative management, the drive to achieve and improve this is what can be called a continuous search for excellence. Take out this hunger and we are left with a sterile management.

Innovation is the introduction of something new which occurs as a result of initiative. Innovation in administration or government thus has some key elements, they are:-

a. A new beneficial idea.
b. Idea generated through initiative.
c. Idea implemented.
d. Such implementation result in beneficial change.
e. Increased organisational effectiveness.

The crucial component is implementation of the idea. It could also be synthesis of two existing ideas. There can be any number of innovations applicable in all walks of administration varying from how to handle habitual late comers or to a complex situation like handling of a state wide employees strike. Innovation can take the form of Transcendental Meditation of Mahershi Mahesh Yogi or the Nano car by Tata or the i-pod etc.

In all cases of innovations what we see is a moving eye looking for opportunities to seize and exploit. It is vital to note that contentment is the greatest enemy of innovation.

Pleasure in the job put perfection in the work.
ARISTOTLE

"Excellence is not a skill. It is an attitude."
RALPH MARSTON

"We are what we repeatedly do. Excellence, then, is not an act, but a habit."
ARISTOTLE

A superior man is modest in his speech, but exceeds in his actions."
CONFUCIUS

"Excellence is the unlimited ability to improve the quality of what you have to offer."
RICK PITINO

"Excellence is in the details. Give attention to the details and excellence will come."

PERRY PAXTON

Find something that you're really interested in doing in your life. Pursue it, set goals, and commit yourself to excellence. Do the best you can."

CHRIS EVERT

"Excellence is doing ordinary things extraordinarily well."

JOHN W. GARDNER

No man ever reached to excellence in any one art or profession without having passed through the slow and painful process of study and preparation.

HORACE

77

Creativity for Every One

Every one can be creative. It is an inborn human talent present in each one of us. It could be a laymen in the street or a small farmer or a grocery shop owner. If they have a will to change and question the way things are being done around, he can do it. Creativity is for every one. What is needed is that the person has

- » Hunger to achieve
- » Necessary knowledge & skills
- » Willingness to put in continuous efforts
- » Self confidence through inner strength & part success.

As administrators and leaders in government it is our responsibility to create a climate, which is open, trusting, helping and demanding this be sustained on a continuous basis by providing a free atmosphere, in the organisation. We need to kindle this fire among employees and reward the creative persons. It is here that the man on top plays a significant role. He and his associates need to constantly nurture it. Deliberate creativity depends on a number of key quilities such as:

1. **Inner drive:** This is first in the order. All others follow. It is a sort of fire that does not normally die in this man's mind. It prods him on and on, and he moves on.
2. **Result orientation:** The individual and organizational drive should give results. These results should be for organisation as a whole. The innovator therefore should fix demanding objectives aligned to the organizational objectives.
3. **Persistence:** An innovator should not give up at the first sign of trouble. He should keep fighting on the predetermined objectives with tenacity and fury.
4. **Inter personal competence:** The ability to get along with boss or peer or subordinates is crucial for successful leaders.
5. **Flexibility:** This is the ability to change pace or even to lie low in certain situations. Instead of getting into a head on collision one should attempt other methods.
6. **Creativity:** This is the drive to create and to build. A constant and continuing drive to do better & to excel. It is the ability to think up and develop new ideas and new way of handling problems that make the innovator what he is and pulls him ahead of the crowd.
7. **Integrity:** It is with integrity one has to succeed and only such success is desirable.

Creativity is inventing, experimenting, growing, taking risks, breaking rules, making mistakes, and having fun."
MARY LOU

"Enthusiasm is excitement with inspiration, motivation, and a pinch of creativity."
BO BENNETT

"Innovation distinguishes between a leader and a follower."
STEVE JOBS

Problems cannot be solved by the same level of thinking that created them."

ALBERT EINSTEIN

"The secret to creativity is knowing how to hide your sources."

ALBERT EINSTEIN

"Creativity is a natural extension of our enthusiasm"

EARL NIGHTINGAL

> As administrators and Leaders in government it is our responsibility to create a climate, which is open, trusting, helping and demanding this be sustained on a continuous basis by providing a free atmosphere, in the organisation. We need to kindle this fire among employees and reward the creative persons.

78

Empower the Team

*M*ore than 90 % of the work force in government comprises of the subordinate executive. They are thus the core personnel who implement our policies. One can appreciate the leverage that can be achieved by suitably empowering this force for they are the ones who are going to make or mar any plan.

In Government we have a typical dichotomical situation, the top and the bottom or the middle levels are not adequately empowered. The situation is more critical at the middle and the lower level of the hierarchy. Employees never receive any training or other inputs that could lead to their professional empowerment which is so crucial to the survival, and growth of government.

Empowerment can be defined as the ability of a team to make decisions about how to do their work and execute them without interference. An empowered team can respond better to the change processes and also make better use of the creative potential of its team. It comes from a combination of factors such as –

1. Members have a sense of self worth.
2. Authority & responsibility to the members for results.
3. Allowing an environment based on trust that can accept honest mistakes.

Empowerment has to be a constant ongoing process in all organisations. A clear manifestation is that the staff enjoys its work. This is significant in government offices where the work processes are repetitive and monotonous. Here the employee's empowerment can be judged by their own initiatives, feedback on improvements and how they assist other team members. This can make individuals step out of the comfort zone in order to assist the team.

Empowering a team can take a great deal of time and efforts of the senior management and leaders. This be done by making the team collectively sit down and find out what all is hampering them from giving their best in the present work environment. This is very significant for block, district and state level which are bogged down by several issues that can be easily resolved to create first a better work place and then a work environment. Such solution that is the outcome of participative process are easily accepted and adopted with ease.

Looking to the fact that the government offices at field level have a small team to work with, the heads of offices can adopt various methods. Some of them can be:

1. **Seek their input** – Staff members can give very valuable practical tips that can be implemented. They are the ones who deal with public on a daily basis and know what will work both internally and externally to make every one happy. By asking all our staff to add input we add value to our staff also.
2. **Positive feedback** – Every individual likes to have a pat on the back for a Job well done. It should be ensured that an appreciation should be promptly communicated. In government we give regular feedback on negative aspect which leads to a demotivated workforce. Positive

feedback helps in developing the loyalty of the employee and should be regularly carried out.
3. **Delegate with authority** – It is important to delegate tasks to individuals and give them specific authority. It would add value to such employee. High performing employees can be given additional responsibility. This would alleviate workload on the head of office and also give employees an opportunity to shine.
4. **Promote employee growth** – A leader in government should look beyond the government by investing time for the human resource. They can be helped in achieving their personal career goals like joining a training programme that would speed up his promotion to next level. Sharing time with them to find out where they want to be in their personal career after 5 years and then help them achieve those goals by providing them necessary assistance can be another option.
5. **Encourage open Communication** – The leaders or heads of offices should clearly communicate the goals and ideas and encourage other heads to do the same. This would create an environment where staff feels comfortable expressing their views and trying new ideas. The staff should be encouraged to contribute their ideas in brain storming sessions and a team mate who has come up with a good idea be not only appreciated but also facilitated to pilot it in a limited manner in the way he has conceived it.

Empowerment should be resorted to on a constant basis so that future leaders can be identified and suitably nurtured. The weekly/fortnightly meetings at office level and the monthly review with senior officers can be an ideal opportunity to do this where a certain time can be slotted for sharing/open house discussions, brain storming. Small teams on various tasks identified by this exchange of ideas can also be formed.

> *As we look ahead into the next century, leaders will be those who empower others.*
>
> BILL GATES

> *"The beauty of empowering others is that your own power is not diminished in the process."*
>
> BARBARA COLOROSE

> *"When you face your fear, most of the time you will discover that it was not really such a big threat after all. We all need some form of deeply rooted, powerful motivation /it empowers us to overcome obstacles so we can live our dreams."*
>
> LES BROWN

Empowerment has to be a constant ongoing process in all organisations. A clear manifestation is that the staff enjoys its work. This is significant in government offices where the work processes are repetitive and monotonous. Here the employee's empowerment can be judged by their own initiatives, feedback on improvements and how they assist other team members.

79

Give New Armaments

Like a war, a leader has to be one up his competitors. He can't fight a 21st century battle with 20th century tools, and weapons. These armaments in our office can be

a. New communication tools, mobile, fax, internet.
b. New courses on self development.
c. New Books.
d. New furniture.
e. New storage system.
f. New work strategies.

We live in a competitive world, particularly in the corporate sector, where the cut throat market strategies lead to merger and acquisition thereby showing the one up manship. To stay in competition it is essential that the entire organisation is updated on the armaments, the tools, the strategies etc at their disposal. In government sector we do not come across that type of situation because there is no competition within the government. However this does not mean that government should not update themselves. In fact it is the constant updation at individual, professional and organizational level that puts the organisation into a constant growth spiral.

Armaments in literal sense means weapon. What are our tools and accessories to deal with the problems

that the system faces at the individual and at the organisational level? In the fast changing scenario in all nations we got to be the latest. **A 21st century war can not be fought with 20th century weapons & strategy.** It has been shown in the Kuwait – Iraq war how the use of modern guided missiles technology could change the face of war on ground and the other side who had not updated itself had no clues to counter that with equal deterrence.

At the organisational level it can take the following shape;

1. **Mental** – It is observed that the intellectual growth of a bureaucrat or a civil servant generally stops once he is selected for a job. Till his selection the individual has to be in a competitive mode but once in, he eases himself. He knows that his Job is secure with the government. It is this feeling that leads to stagnating mental thought. It is very important for each employee at every level to keep his mind sharp by reading, writing and learning new skills. Extensive reading exposes the mind to new ideas which result in generation of creative thoughts.

The intellectual upgradation at senior leadership level should be of serious nature involving efforts to imbibe and learn new skills. This can be in the form of taking study leave to do a new degree course or taking time off and undertake a short term 3-4 week course or some specific aspect that leads to his professional improvement, say taking a course in new accounting system, learning Oracle or D-base systems etc. Giving new armaments is like updating your computer with the latest version of software. Leaders should always be on the lookout for new & improved leadership tools and resources that add value. Those tools should be such that focus on influencing the leader and his team.

Stephen Covey in his book The '7 Habits of Highly Effective People' has used the word 'sharpen the saw'. He has talked that by reviewing the four dimensions of your nature – physical, spiritual, mental and social/emotional, you can work more quickly and effortlessly and to do this one need to be proactive in his approach.

The physical dimension: It involves caring for your physical body-eating the right foods, taking rest and regular exercising. Regular exercising keeps our body and mind adequately toned up to deal comfortably to the work related stresses. An active and energetic person would also exude better body language confidence than a person with a sedentary type of work schedule.

The spiritual dimension: It is the centre of our value system. It uplifts us to timeless truth of humanity. By carefully examining what life is ultimately all about and what are our leadership centres, we can reassume and recharge our missions.

The mental dimension: The mind can be kept sharp by reading, writing, organising and planning. By dedicating at least one hour every day for our physical, mental and spiritual development we can keep these faculties alert.

The social/Emotional dimension: Our emotional life is primarily developed out of and manifested in our relationships with others. Renewing it requires focus and exercise in our interaction with others. By helping others in a meaningful way each day we increase our deposits of love.

> *The best weapon of a dictatorship is secrecy, but the best weapon of a democracy should be the weapon of openness"*
> — NIELS BOHR

> *I know not with what weapons World War III will be fought, but World War IV will be fought with sticks and stones.*
> — ALBERT EINSTEIN

220 *Leadership in Government*

"Ideas are more powerful than guns. We would not let our enemies have guns, why should we let them have ideas."

Joseph Stalin

"The main foundations of every state, new states as well as ancient or composite ones, are good laws and good arms – you cannot have good laws without good arms, and where there are good arms, good laws inevitably follow"

Niccolo Machiavelli

Any tool is a weapon if you hold it right.

Ani DiFranco

Education is the most powerful weapon which you can use to change the world.

Nelson Mandela

Armaments in literal sense means weapon. What are our tools and accessories to deal with the problems that the system faces at the individual and at the organisational level? In the fast changing scenario in all nations we got to be the latest. A 21st century war can not be fought with 20th century weapons & strategy.

80

Awards & Rewards

*A*s *part of my dissertation work for the MBA degree I chose the topic of organizational development.One of its aspect was to study the top 5 things which district heads value as motivators in public services. The results were amazing. Out of more than 100 district heads who responded, the majority gave non monitory rewards the maximum score.*

The importance of incentives: Rewards and awards are grossly under utilized in all governments. Wherever they do exist they are largely for soft components which are difficult to quantify and political influence in choosing the persons is always there. Government lacks a system of constant and continuous mechanism of appreciating the good work done. Work more – Perk more, philosophy is not followed in government.

Show that you care with rewards: Rewards and awards in general are grossly underutilized in all government departments. **Getting rewards in government system is a rarity now. The reason for this lies in the myth that the employee is supposed to work with 100% or even more dedication because he is paid for it, so he can not ask for being rewarded for doing something extra ordinary. It has been observed on several occasions where an individual's case**

for award or rewards is scuttled for the reason that the person was doing his normal duty. **This type of attitude breeds only average and sub-averages persons who work for 7 or 8 hours and not work for a cause, vision or a mission.** No wonder we have almost every government employee starved of appropriate motivation. Awards and rewards are an excellent way to motivate or cheer up the individual for doing a good Job.

Apart from recognising them as responsible individual in the system reward makes all employees a direct stakeholder. This is something that needs to be increased at least a hundred times. It's a myth that all awards, rewards or incentives cost money. A simple letter of appreciation or a certificate of recognition can do wonder.

The private or the corporate sector has a direct way of calculating what an individual has done and looking to the competition of open economies, the boss has a stake in ensuring that his team continues to perform above the goals set. Here the goals are generally well quantifiable. Government sector has this problem of performance evaluation. Generally it is difficult to quantify the worth of the Job done by a civil servant in one day or a week. This is primarily due to the nature of the job, not that it can not be quantified.

The question of rewards or incentives has also drawn the attention of the 6th pay commission set up the by Government of India. The commission in its report submitted in March 2008 has talked about "Performance Related Incentive Scheme". Under the Scheme employees will be eligible for pecuniary remuneration over and above the pay. The scheme is designed to be budget neutral. This is a welcome move by government of India. We can hope that this scheme can bring about a major shift in the motivational level of government employees.

Work more – Perk more: In government we lack a system of constant & continuous mechanism of appreciating the good work done. The country is today at a Juncture where it has to compete with countries like China. It is time that we move to a rewards based system. Let each individual be rewarded in direct proportion to the results he gets. Such on approach can bring about:

* Project being completed on time.
* Saving on cost over run.
* A spirit of healthy competition at all levels.
* Each one getting paid additional reward on the basis of his performance.
* Improvement in quantity as well as quality of output as he is also going to work for himself.
* Bring focus on accomplishment rather than on activity.
* People are going to be output focussed and would be willing to go that extra mile or take the extra pains.

Other ways to award:

Though money is one ways of increasing the Job performance it isn't the only one. Employees can be rewarded, in other ways too, such as;

1. **Give a special assignment** – An employee can be given new challenging assignment and in the process letting every one know that you value him. It will stimulate him.
2. **Provide him high visibility** – The present generation appreciates this. Everyone wants to be acknowledged for

doing a good Job. And all it takes from you is to offer praise publically, say in a staff meeting or via e-mail tell the key personnel about the individual's accomplishment. It is free, easy and well received by every one.

3. **Send them on a training programme of their choice** – The performer's skills & capabilities can be enhanced by sending them for further short term course to an institute of his choice, on subject which he wishes to undertake. If such courses are held at some exotic places, it can give the employees an additional boost. Interacting with diverse groups can be a great motivator and once these employees are back, they would be a great resource to the organisation.

4. **Provide feedback** – It is very important for employees to know how they are doing in their Jobs. We can invite them for a lunch and ask them whether they have any questions or need help with their work. This opportunity can be used to provide feedback on their performance. Praise them for doing a good Job. All such opportunities should be used to let them know how they are doing so that they are better able to respond to your needs & the needs of the deportment.

5. **Celebrate their successes** – Whenever an employee or a group achieves a landmark, celebrate it. The group will appreciate the recognition and you will appreciate the loyalty that comes in return.

Recognising employees is not just a nice thing for people it is also a communication tool that reinforces a certain type of employees' behavior which you want to be repeated. Such employee recognition system is simple, immediate and powerfully reinforcing.

I hope for the best, it's great to be nominated even once in your life."

CHRISTINA AGUILERA

Awards are wonderful. I've been nominated many times and I've won many awards. But my journey is not towards that. If it happens it will be a blast. If it doesn't, it's still been a blast.

TOM CRUISE

"Don't worry when you are not recognized, but strive to be worthy of recognition."

ABRAHAM LINCOLN

"In the arena of human life the honors and rewards fall to those who show their good qualities in action."

ARISTOTLE

"There are two things people want more than sex and money – recognition and praise."

MARY KAY ASH

"Work is not man's punishment. It is his reward and his strength and his pleasure."

GEORGE SAND

"I can accept failure, but, I can't accept not trying."

MICHAEL JORDAN

"Today, and every day, deliver more than you are getting paid to do. The victory of success will be half won when you learn the secret of putting out more than is expected in all that you do. Make yourself so valuable in your work that eventually you will become indispensable. Exercise your privilege to go the extra mile, and enjoy all the rewards you receive. You deserve them!"

OG MANDINO

"Men are rich only as they give. He who gives great service gets great rewards."

ELBERT HUBBARD

A word of encouragement during a failure is worth more than an hour of praise after success.

ANONYMOUS

Appreciation is a wonderful thing. It makes what is excellent in others belong to us as well.

VOLTAIRE

Flatter me, and I may not believe you. Criticize me, and I may not like you. Ignore me, and I may not forgive you. Encourage me, and I may not forget you.

WILLIAM ARTHUR

> Getting rewards in government system in a rarity now. The reason for this lies in the myth that the employee is supposed to work with 100% or even more dedication because he is paid for it, so he can not ask for being rewarded for doing something extra ordinary. It has been observed on several occasions where an individual's case for award or rewards is scuttled for the reason that the person was doing his normal duty. This type of attitude breeds only average and sub-averages persons who work for 7 or 8 hours and not work for a cause, vision or a mission.

81

Perform

We should give results and not excuses as government is all about performance. **All leaders should therefore aim at betterment in performance.** It is performance only that wins the heart and mind of common man and it is performance only that would lead to growth. **All leadership skill and qualities would take us no where if it does not result in growth in concrete outputs.** It could be increased productivity or more profit or any other measurable parameter. Thus leadership is all about performing on critical issues entrusted to government.

In government system there are so many things through which a leader and his followers can deliver. To illustrate a few –

1. A Revenue official in districts delivers by deciding innumerable revenue and executive matters in his capacity as a revenue court.
2. A Station House Officer can deliver by promptly conducting enquiry into various reports which are lodged at his police station.
3. A District Agriculture officer can deliver by maximizing timely distribution of agricultural inputs like seed,

pesticide and fertilizer to farmers during Rabi and Kharif season so that they don't have to run around.
4. The district civil supplies officer delivers by ensuring that the stocks of various consumer products are available for issue at fair price shops for the common citizen who goes there to buy his monthly ration.
5. The engineers perform by ensuring that the various construction projects are finished on time.
6. The engineer perform when the water from irrigation canal to the cultivator's fields reaches on time and there are no conflicts on distribution of water among cultivators.
7. The local police perform when traffic rules are observed and one is not struck in long jams.

These diverse illustration have been written to draw home a point that there is huge potential for all of us to perform and bring happiness to million of citizens.

Performance in government is an interdependent activity. It has a chain reaction effect on other associated and even unassociated activities. For example higher generation of power by power station means that there are lesser power cut and black outs in villages. It also means that more water is pumped into agricultural fields resulting in higher agricultural production and profits to farmers. The chain reaction has a multiplier effect down the line.

Another illustration can be efficient performance of duty by the police department which results in lesser traffic violation, lesser road accidents resulting in greater discipline in city. A quite peaceful situation favours coming up of new industrial units in such area. It is a known fact that industries are vary of going to places where law and order situation is not good. To illustrate how the silent bureaucracy plays a vital role in the life of an individual, take the case of grant of visa to go abroad. The application may have to go through the following stages:

1. Procure form from web or passport office.
2. Fill up and send to your boss and seek a no objection.
3. Send it to the nodal department/Ministry for their clearance.
4. Seek no objection of department of economic affairs.
5. Seek political clearance from External affairs Ministry.
6. Submit papers to Embassy.
7. Collect Visa from the outsourced agency.

The same can be repeated for obtaining Gun license from Collectors office or getting permission for medical treatment outside the country. In fact there are innumerable illustrations where grass root governance is seen in action. One can imagine the satisfaction and goodwill an officer or an office generates if it responds promptly to the matter at hand.

The Business of Government is to make life comfortable for its citizens through its processes of governance. It is through these small acts spread over hundreds of offices and affecting life of millions of people that a government shows its success or failure. It is the public face of government. A common citizen may find the system slow, corrupt and inefficient in deliverance and thereby bring disrepute to the government at helm or may find a prompt, smiling, supportive, facilitative functionary in office ready to complete his job in time. The leaders have to create such transparent and efficient team of subordinate functionaries and through them disseminate the message of governance.

There is a common tendency to equate industrial scenario with the performance of bureaucratic offices like say a District Treasury, A Municipal Commissioners office, an agriculture extension office, Superintendent of police or a post master. These are all offices where in real terms you do not have a production line, heavy machines and computer controlled system but you have a small team of 5 to 12 people working on files which move from one table to another and some time at the end of the day accompany to his house or on flight to some city where the person is going on tour. A leader in government has to pay attention to all these minor cogs in the larger wheel called government for it is these millions of small nuts and bolts that give strength to the body structure of government. It is therefore of paramount significance that what is done in government gets measured. Today we can develop tools and system that can measure almost every activity be it the bureaucratic or otherwise.

> *It's the action, not the fruit of the action, that's important. You have to do the right thing. It may not be in your power, may not be in your time, that there will be any fruit. But that doesn't mean you stop doing the right thing. You may never know what results come from your action. But if you do nothing, there will be no result.*
>
> M.K. GANDHI

"*Practice as if you are the worst; perform as if you are the best.*"

"*Don't lower your expectations to meet your performance. Raise your level of performance to meet your expectations. Expect the best of yourself, and then do what is necessary to make it a reality.*"

RALPH MARSTON

"*Performance stands out like a ton of diamonds. Non performance can always be explained away.*"

HAROLD S. GENEEN

"The thing about performance, even if it's only an illusion, is that it is a celebration of the fact that we do contain within ourselves infinite possibilities."
SYDNEY SMITH

"An ounce of performance is worth more than a pound of preachment"
ELBERT HUBBARD

"When performance exceeds ambition, the overlap is called success"
CULLEN HIGHTOWER

"Leadership is not magnetic personality/that can just as well be a glib tongue. It is not making friends and influencing people/that is flattery. Leadership is lifting a person's vision to higher sights, the raising of a person's performance to a higher standard, the building of a personality beyond its normal limitations."
PETER F. DRUCKER

All leaders should therefore aim at betterment in performance. It is performance only that wins the heart and mind of common man and it is performance only that would lead to growth. All leadership skill and qualities would take us no where if it does not result in growth in concrete outputs.

82

Motivated Work Force – The Charge That Generates the Force

Every boss complains about employees not being adequately charged, not being adequately committed or being involved in what is happening around them or about what they are expected to do. **As leaders it is very vital that our work force is motivated and dedicated.** Motivation is a tool that can be developed and used for every employee. **Only when they are motivated can the leaders show results and perform well. Motivation is intrinsic in all human beings. What the leader or the manager has to do is to identify within the ambit of defined job, as to what he likes best to do in his work.** Managers, administrator or supervisor all need it and all need to align themselves with the overall vision, mission, and goals of the organsation. However, as leaders we can find what the employees are looking for in their tasks, what is that moves them or they are passionate about. Once this can be identified and the tasks relocated we can have a team that is doing their respective jobs in a highly motivated and devoted manner.

As an illustration, in the public hospital team of 50 senior professionals there can be some who likes research, other likes clinical work and another lot is enthusiastic about personnel matters. By selectively giving responsibility to persons on jobs or tasks they are best at, a charged and motivated team can be created. It will be a task they would be doing for their inner satisfaction. By providing them selective training their competencies can be further improved. It would further charge him on the motivational path. This can be tried out at different levels of government. It may not always be possible that you could assign a specific task to a specific person, but even 40 or 60% reallocations of tasks within the organisation can be considered as excellent. Getting to know the core competencies of each employee is a time consuming consultative process and can best be done by a collective briefing followed by a written feed back on a given set of question relating to the task they are performing.

Motivation is not a single stroke or single stage activity. It is something that needs to be reaffirmed on a continuous basis, both internally and externally. The internal motivation is an activity that would need effort of the individual to recharge him whereas the external motivation would be carried out by the organisation. It could be sending him for a refresher course or giving him a reward for doing excellent job.

A team which has the freedom of applying new ideas for betterment of the organisation definitely attracts motivated people creating innovative thinking. Its application across the organisations by spirited supervisors, bosses, and leaders recharges the innovative mind. Innovation is something that has to be continued in all organisations at all levels and when such innovation is emerging out of spirited team across the organisations it leads to motivated workforce. A motivated team always yields better outcome be it disposal of files or timeliness or conducting certain number of field trials for a project.

Motivation is a positive act and it needs positive efforts by the organisation. It could be;

1. Better work place amenities.
2. Better salaries and other perks.
3. Other performance related rewards.
4. Regular letter of appreciation to those who have done well.

I have observed interacting with thousands of employees over the past 28 years that what they seek from their government or supervisors is not a fortune. The things which they feel can make them more productive are simple and affordable. A letter of appreciation or a simple phone call to cheer him up can do wonder.

To finish first, you must first finish.

RICK MEARS

Thinking is the hardest work there is, which is the probable reason so few engage in it.

HENRY FORD

The best motivating is self-motivating. The guy says," I wish someone would come by and turn me on." What if they don't show up? You've got to have a better plan for your life.

JIM ROHN

There is work that is work and there is play that is play; there is play that is work and work that is play. And in only one of these lies happiness.

GELETT BURGESS

There is only one way... to get anybody to do anything. And that is by making the other person want to do it.

DALE CARNEGIE

There's no substitute for hard work.

THOMAS EDISON

Motivated Work Force – The Charge That Generates the Force

We know where most of the creativity, the innovation, the stuff that drives productivity lies – in the minds of those closest to the work.
                                    JACK WELCH

What is written without effort is in general read without pleasure.
                                    SAMUEL JOHNSON

Small opportunities are often the beginning of great enterprises.
                                    DEMOSTHENES

Success seems to be connected with action. Successful people keep moving. They make mistakes, but they don't quit.
                                    CONRAD HILTON

Successful leaders have the courage to take action while others hesitate.
                                    JOHN C. MAXWELL

> As leaders it is very vital that our work force is motivated and dedicated. Motivation is a tool that can be developed and used for every employee. Only when they are motivated can the leaders show results and perform well. Motivation is intrinsic in all human beings. What the leader or the manager has to do is to identify within in the ambit of defined job, as to what he likes best to do in his work.

83

Getting Out of the Comfort Zone

It is the law of nature that we all tend to reach a state of least energy – the most comfortable state. **To do anything which changes the status quo needs additional energy to take you to the higher levels. Whether it is giving more output in terms of work or any other situation we all know that human being have a tendency to take the route of least resistance. It is this attitude what is called the zone of comfort.**

In an organization in transformational mode such comfort zones have no permanent place. The leaders in government should always need to keep an eye on their team and ensure that they are not sliding back into the comfort zone. If the leader himself slides to this zone rest assure that the entire office would also fall back into this state very soon. Leaders in government need to be watchful about this tendency.

The institutions of government are such that they never sleep. Governments never sleep, with them lies the responsibility that every citizen has a comfortable sleep at the end of the day. Literally it can be seen with government in action at:

» Power Boards
» The Police department

Getting Out of the Comfort Zone

- » The Security Forces
- » The Civil Aviation, Shipping and Railways
- » Water supply and sanitation etc.

Some of these are sovereign functions of government and if we allow these to get into the comfort zone the common man in villages and towns would suffer.

To keep the employees and the organisation out of the slackness phase the goals have to be kept slightly stretched. The stretched goals (though achievable) make the team down the line think and work on new innovative ways to achieve those slightly stretched goals. The slackness in government systems and sliding into the comfort zone can some time prove disastrous for the system or the organisation at large. We can see plenty of such examples around us.

A scholar who cherishes the love of comfort is not fit to be deemed a scholar.
                                                                LAO-TZU

We shall have no better conditions in the future if we are satisfied with all those which we have at present.
                                                                THOMAS EDISON

A dream is your creative vision for your life in the future. You must break out of your current comfort zone and become comfortable with the unfamiliar and the unknown.
                                                                DENIS WAITLEY

If you remain in your comfort zone you will not go any further.
                                                                CATHERINE PULSIFER

We cannot become what we want to be by remaining what we are.
                                                                MAX DEPREE

Nobody ever died of discomfort, yet living in the name of comfort has killed more ideas, more opportunities, more actions, and more growth than everything else combined. Comfort kills!
                                                                T. HARV EKER

If you put yourself in a position where you have to stretch outside your comfort zone, then you are forced to expand your consciousness.
LES BROWN

"Move out of your comfort zone. You can only grow if you are willing to feel awkward and uncomfortable when you try something new."
BRIAN TRACY

If you're in a comfort zone, afraid to venture out, Remember that all winners were at one time filled with doubt.
AUTHOR UNKNOWN,

Life loses its meaning when we get stuck up in comfort zone.
M.K. SONI

To do anything which changes the status quo needs additional energy to take you to the higher levels. Whether it is giving more output in terms of work or any other situation we all know that human being have a tendency to take the route of least resistance. It is this attitude what is called the zone of comfort.

84

Evaluate

Performance of organisations and offices needs to be constantly evaluated. Whereas definite systems of assessing as to what is happening in an industrial unit in the private/corporate world exist, questions have repeatedly been raised that governments are not able to evolve some concrete method of evaluating its performance. Profits in balance sheet are a clear indicator in private sector but there is nothing so specific in government services. Most of our government offices are service oriented which need to be provided efficiently. Thus whatever we intend to deliver should have the quality aspect taken care of. This means that effectiveness in achieving policy outcomes be monitored.

Evaluating any programme needs the baseline information of performance of previous years or some other reference against which the performance could be judged. Setting bench marks is a process that has to be done keeping the state/national goal in mind as it is related to the budgetary allocations. Goal setting at the beginning of the year or an intermediate stage helps in comparative evaluation. Based on them necessary corrective steps can be taken in achieving the goals. Goal setting also enhance intra and inter organisational communication.

Internally it tells the staff what is expected from them and externally they can know what cooperation would be needed from others.

Thus performance measurement

1. Puts goals in focus.
2. Is a way to communicate with the organisation.
3. Provides time for other strategic planning to those in position of leadership.

Public expects accountability in government. Monitoring the performance gives us criteria to differentiate success from failure. It also results in less of wastages because we know where the organisation is going to & thereby devotes energy to focused results. Monitoring the performance can thus result in better decision making thereby improving internal accountability to the organisation and external accountability to the public. It also becomes a tool for strategic planning.

"True genius resides in the capacity for evaluation of uncertain, hazardous, and conflicting information"
WINSTON CHURCHILL

"Everything that can be counted does not necessarily count; everything that counts cannot necessarily be counted"
ALBERT EINSTEIN

"One of the great mistakes is to judge policies and programs by their intentions rather than their results"
MILTON FRIEDMAN

"First get your facts; then you can distort them at your leisure"
MARK TWAIN

"I know that half of my advertising dollars are wasted ... I just don't know which half"
JOHN WANAMAKER

"Fear cannot be banished, but it can be calm and without panic; it can be mitigated by reason and evaluation"

VANNEVAR BUSH

Evaluating any programme needs the baseline information of performance of previous years or some other reference against which the performance could be judged. Setting bench marks is a process that has to be done keeping the state/national goal in mind as it is related to the budgetary allocations. Goal setting at the beginning of the year or an intermediate stage helps in comparative evaluation.

85

Tapping the Untapped Potential –
Releasing the Power of Hanuman

We know Ramayana and the story of Hanuman. He always had immense power to do the apparently most impossible things but he was unaware of his inner strengths. However once he realised his power and when that immense power was aimed at the mission in a focused manner, we all know the successful results. Governments are also like Hanuman, having immense untapped potential. It is the leader who has to identify those areas where the organisation needs additional energy and also to identify the persons who have that power house called Hanuman.

Where is this power hidden amongst the millions of government employees and who would identify and channelise this energy? This is what the leader is meant to be. Identifying the right powerhouses and positioning them appropriately. Though there are no studies to authenticate it, but from the experience I can say that the realised potential of a civil servant may be only 15 to 20%. Where has the other energy gone? Is he not working for the mandatory 7 hours per day? The answer is that it is not for how many hours one is working but what is significant and crucial is as to what is he working for? It is mere activity or does that activity yields results? Is he doing things right or doing the right things? It should be the aim of leaders to produce effective teams-teams that show results.

It is the organisation leader who has to ensure that the wastages of energy are minimised and at the same time maximise existing energies by synergy and harmony. Synergy is something all organisation need, more so for governmental organisation where multiplicity of agencies need to be coordinated and diversity of systems to be synergised. It is strengthening the inter departmental activities which can increase the output many fold. Using the untapped potential is something that has to be done on a continuous basis. As we grow the Hanuman also grows, so in real term the gap would always remain and there would always be more to do to keep the god happy.

The exercise in harvesting the untapped potential is the job of a leader. He has to transform and do it not in the notional sense but transform it in such a manner that it brings transformation at all levels. The most interesting aspect of this untapped potential is that it is always there, you just have to unravel it. It does not need any additional resources to tap this 80% gap, just the attitudinal changes, would get it. An example can be;

Raise crop production by 100% in just one crop cycle.

This is an example where just by proper marshaling of the inputs for that crop and by scientific timely intervention the crop output can be doubled. It has happened in Madhya Pradesh. The soil always had the nutrients, what it needed was

» Timely soil preparation.
» Appropriate seed selection.

- » Appropriate time of sowing.
- » Fertilizers, insecticide and pesticides used along scientific lines.
- » Inter cropping.
- » Training to formers.
- » Appropriate watering.

Interestingly all those interventions are not cost intensive, they are basically related to mindset and attitude. This is an example where the farmers have shown that they have a hidden energy and the government joined hand to get the maximum out of it.

This change of mindset of chasing the targets to performing your natural self is the role of the leader and to inculcate in them the feeling that they can do it. Chasing targets is externally driven whereas performing your natural self is internally driven. We have innumerable examples where the unbelievable have been achieved by appropriate strategic intervention. These show the power of people. Those who are on the receiving end and those who have to deliver. I have noticed that once the two sides realise this win- win situation their outcome is mind boggling.

Everyone has inside himself a piece of good news! The good news is that you really don't know how great you can be, how much you can love, what you can accomplish, and what your potential is!

Our strength often increases in proportion to the obstacles imposed upon it.

PAUL DE RAPIN

Joy comes from using your potential.

WILL SCHULTZ

The greatest crime in the world is not developing your potential. When you do what you do best, you are helping not only yourself, but the world.

ROGER WILLIAMS

The will to win, the desire to succeed, the urge to reach your full potential... these are the keys that will unlock the door to personal excellence.

EDDIE ROBINSON

Knowledge is only potential power.

NAPOLEON HILL

It's not what you've got; it's what you use that makes a difference.

ZIG ZIGLAR

The potential of the average person is like a huge ocean unsailed, a new continent unexplored, a world of possibilities waiting to be released and channeled toward some great good.

BRIAN TRACY

The wise man looks into space and he knows there is no limited dimension.

LAO-TZU

"The only way to discover the limits of the possible is to go beyond them into the impossible."

ARTHUR C CLARKE

Where is this power hidden amongst the millions of government employees and who would identify and channelise this energy? This is what the leader is meant to be. Identifying the right powerhouses and positioning them appropriately.

86
The Team that Works –
Selecting the Right Person

Like all organisation governments too need proper selection of personnel and then appropriate deployment. Unlike the corporate world the choice of staff in government set up is limited. The limiting factor could be the qualification, training or the attitude. Though one can have a pool of large persons available in any department, the choice of posting according to the appropriateness of the skills is not always an easy task. Nevertheless, heads of organisation can constitute the mission teams by suitable mix of aptitude, training and skills. This exercise may take 2-3 months and some time one may not get a person of the right requirement due to its non-availability and one may have to use whatever limited resource the office has. It is the discretion of the head of office to allocate what work is assigned to whom. Those who have the fire to work and deliver at the pace can be given key assignments.

The selection of persons has to be attuned to the job needs and the strategy. The persons should be aligned with organisational goals. The team can be given performance based incentives so that they remain always charged up. Every office needs to devise some

human resource policy which has the mechanism of constant rewards and incentives to those who are good performers.

Choosing the team and their appropriate positioning is a leadership activity and needs to be carried out seriously. It may take some time but that patience is worth it. It is important to keep in mind that the team should have sound professional competence and comprise of persons who can deliver with passion.

> *"Individually, we are one drop. Together, we are an ocean."*
> — RYUNOSUKE

> *"Coming together is a beginning. Keeping together is progress. Working together is success."*
> — HENRY FORD

> *"Talent wins games, but teamwork and intelligence wins championships."*
> — MICHAEL JORDAN

> *Teamwork: Simply stated, it is less me and more we.*
> — UNKNOWN

> *No one can whistle a symphony. It takes an orchestra to play it.*
> — H.E. LUCCOCK

> *"Coming together is a beginning.*
> *Keeping together is progress.*
> *Working together is success."*
> — HENRY FORD

> *"Michael, if you can't pass, you can't play."*
> — COACH DEAN SMITH

> *"We must all hang together, or assuredly, we shall all hang separately."*
> — BENJAMIN FRANKLIN

The selection of persons has to be attuned to the job needs and the strategy. The persons should be aligned with organisational goals. The team can be given performance based incentives so that they remain always charged up. Every office needs to devise some human resource policy which has the mechanism of constant rewards and incentives to those who are good performers.

87

Our Everyday Heros

Governance is a complex and continuous process which has been going on since ages in all societies. It is being developed by small leaders who resides in all of us, such as

1. The good deals that we do when we promptly do a job.
2. The services we provide which brings a smile on our customer's face.
3. When we provide a helping hand in suggesting solutions, even when we are not part of the solution.

It's the attitude that makes a person a leader of his group. We should look for these unsung performers around us and develop them. This would help creating a healthy environment in the organization.

I think of a hero as someone who understands the degree of responsibility that comes with his freedom.
Everyone is necessarily the hero of his own life story.

BOB DYLAN

A hero is no braver than an ordinary man, but he is braver five minutes longer.

JOHN BARTH

"If everybody was satisfied with himself there would be no heroes."

MARK TWAIN

The ordinary man is involved in action, the hero acts. An immense difference.

HENRY MILLER

"The hero is one who kindles a great light in the world, who sets up blazing torches in the dark streets of life for men to see by."

FELIX ADLER

88

Let Each Individual Be Accountable

Every day we hear people talking about lack of accountability in public services, about discussions on time and cost overrun of projects of vital importance and yet none taking the responsibility for losses of public money. In fact it can be seen in all government offices. Instances could be,

- A stalled construction project.
- Enquiries going on for years.
- Cases pending for years before various judicial, quasi-judicial or executive bodies and no decision in sight.
- Officials not available to carryout the work they are paid for.

People are talking about accountability of public servants who had been entrusted with a certain task and for which he gets paid for.

Accountability means to be answerable for the acts of omissions or commissions that result in certain things happening in a certain way. Accountability also means;

1. To be responsible for whatever is happening (good or bad) under a person's command.

2. To stand up and take credit for the positive things that is happening in the organisation.

In large organisations, like the government departments, it is essential that the top, middle and the lower level executives are entrusted with certain goals and targets which they must fulfill. Regular review by seniors either weekly or monthly can motivate and charge them to deal with the organisational issues head on. A motivated team is always found to be more accountable. By making regular review it can be found as to where the problem exists and who are the non-performers? If they are not willing to improve they are removed from the assignment which they are not suited to.

Accountability should be one of the main corner stone of the administration. By overt expression of displeasure for non performers and creating conditions that encourages staff, a very healthy environment can be created. Government organisations being megasized it is important that the goal setting be done by written instructions. Of late some departments like Health & Family Welfare and Education have also introduced performance linked incentives where the performance is measured by output in relation to prescribed services standard. In public services related system it can be strengthened by the mechanism of transparency in government processes. Accountability and transparency have a mutually reinforcing effect. The free flow of information within and outside the organisation also helps reduce corruption.

By making government working accessible to the public scrutiny we can ensure that adequate mechanism develops in all organisations against mis use. India in the past few years has made rapid progress in opening up the government functioning to general public. The right to information act has been extremely useful in making important documents accessible. Public armed with relevant papers has brought about several changes in government functioning.

Till the onset of 21st Century our country was governed by the Official Secret Act 1923 which had virtually made every paper in government a secret document. There had been innumerable instances in the past where a person was penalised for having copies of some insignificant government papers which may or may not be related to him. The secretive nature of governments and its officers till the 21st Century had been one of the reasons of poor accountability. There had been tendencies to hide information from public. The legislative and other changes brought about in all major states have started the processes of bringing in transparency in public offices. Right to Information Act 2005, citizen charters have been of great help in these efforts.

"Accountability breeds response-ability."

STEPHEN R. COVEY

"It is not only what we do, but also what we do not do, for which we are accountable."

MOLIERE

We are accountable for our decisions in our personal life so why shouldn't we be just as accountable in our work life."

CATHERINE PULSIFER

"You are accountable for your actions, your decisions, your life; no one else is, but you."

CATHERINE PULSIFIER

"God does not want us to do extraordinary things; He wants us to do ordinary things extraordinarily well."

BISHOP GORE

Let Each Individual Be Accountable

"Some favorite expressions of adults: "It's not my job... No one told me... It couldn't be helped." True freedom begins and ends with personal accountability."

DAN ZADRA

"Thinking well is wise; planning well, wiser; doing well wisest and best of all."

PERSIAN PROVERB

"The way to gain a good reputation is to endeavor to be what you desire to be."

SOCRATES

"Success is more permanent when you achieve it without destroying your principles."

WALTER CRONKITE

"If you have integrity, nothing else matters; if you don't have integrity, nothing else matters."

ALAN SIMPSON

In large organisations, like the government departments, it is essential that the top, middle and the lower level executives are entrusted with certain goals and targets which they must fulfill. Regular review by seniors either weekly or monthly can motivate and charge them to deal with the organisational issues head on. A motivated team is always found to be more accountable. By making regular review it can be found as to where the problem exists and who are the non-performers?

89

Stay Fit

There is a very old saying that if you lose money you lose nothing but if you lose health you lose everything. It beautifully summarises the significance of good health. In the demanding 21st Century competitive scenario with good pay and perks it is essential that all of us not only earn but also enjoy the fruit of hard labour by having good health. Overweight, high blood pressure, diabetes, high cholesterol, heart ailments are some of the diseases that are linked to prosperity of a dynamic and 'A' type personality executive. All leaders need to keep excellent health only then can they give their best to the job and also get the best out of their team.

Good health and fitness are not a very difficult task and all of us can achieve it with case. We have all read Anil Ambani jogging 10 km every day along with his team. Good health is not merely about your own well being, it also exudes positive radiation in the environment which you occupy. Good health also keeps your body and soul in harmony to produce streams of new innovative ideas. Spending a little time of 30 to 50 minutes per day can rejuvenate yourself and keep you fully charged to keep pace on the unchartered path of administrative jungles.

Our body if not properly looked after depreciates faster than an industrial plant or machinery. As leaders we should be concerned about not only our own health but also all the employees who work with us. Just like a good machine needs regular servicing, we need to maintain our body vehicle in a state of constant fitness. Some very simple things that can be started by everybody at any stage are:

1. Go for early morning or evening brisk walk for 1/2 an hour.
2. Do 15-20 minutes of daily meditation or yogic Asans, it really rejuvenates you.
3. Play a light or vigorous game suitable to your body capacity. Table Tennis, Lawn Tennis, Billiards, Badminton, are a few club or group games that can be played on a regular basis. One can have a game suited to ones body.
4. Eat light and fibrous foods.
5. Have regular night sleep of 6 to 7 hours.
6. Take brief breaks between the work cycles of 2-3 hour for 10-15 minutes.
7. Walk as much as possible during the work hour i.e. walking between 2 buildings or going from ground floor to 2nd floor.
8. Plan work in such a manner that you are not stressed about time in office.
9. Get regular health check ups to keep track of your weight, lipids, blood pressure, total blood picture etc.

There may be situation where your health check up reveals that one or more then one tests have some abnormality. In such situation prompt medical consultations be done to bring the blood pressure, lipids or other blood picture back to normal. Timely attention to executive stress can get us prompt relief from later stage complication like depression, insomnia, headache, backache, etc.

It is ideal to involve your wife or other family members in walks or playing games, it really creates a very positive effect on mind and body apart from improving the inter personal bondages, so vital to a healthy family life.

Fitness is not a one time mantra. It is something that has to be practiced on a daily basis all through your life. It should become a part of your daily routine like food, drink and sleep. Today we have a large number of books available which can advise us on various aspects of our health, during different phases of our life. These books written by reputed authors are of immense help and should be used as regular supplement to your other reading material.

Keeping good health is not a difficult task. Just being conscious about observing certain discipline and being regular on certain exercises can do wonder. Stay fit and enjoys the fruits of your hard work.

Work consists of whatever a body is obliged to do. Play consists of whatever a body is not obliged to do.

MARK TWAIN

Work is man's most natural form of relaxation.

DAGOBERT D. RUNES

A sad soul can kill you quicker than a germ.

JOHN STEINBECK

Love cures people—both the ones who give it and the ones who receive it.

DR KARL MENNINGER

The greatest wealth is health.

VIRGIL

He who has health has hope; and he who has hope has everything.

ARABIAN PROVERB

A good laugh and a long sleep are the best cures in the doctor's book.

IRISH PROVERB

When it comes to eating right and exercising, there is no "I'll start tomorrow." Tomorrow is disease.

TERRI GUILLEMETS

Health and cheerfulness naturally beget each other.

JOSEPH ADDISON

Fitness is not a one time mantra. It is something that has to be practiced on a daily basis all through your life. It should become a part of your daily routine like food, drink and sleep. Today we have a large number of books available which can advise us on various aspects of our health, during different phases of our life. These books written by reputed authors are of immense help and should be used as regular supplement to your other reading material.

90
Efficiency at Work

Government offices and systems are invariably complained about its slow pace and corruption. In fact the two are interrelated. It is often said that the whole administrative system is run to meet its own ends and various schemes too are run to satisfy those ends. The constitutional protections given to civil servants regarding their removal from service had been provided to make the civil services apolitical otherwise we would have a situation where the change of government would also have seen thousands of employees being removed and new and political workers appointed. The civil service gives permanence and continuity to administration. With sixth Pay Commission report recommending a further hike in the salary packages of civil servants, the issue of efficiency and effectiveness has assumed greater significance. Public needs to know why the employees are paid more? In the present day world we have put various arrangements in place that has made office work easier compared to the situation some decades ago. The data management system, the computers, and modern tools of review and monitoring can be used to do the job in a more efficient manner.

A leader has to see that the offices use modern office system that makes the delivery of services faster, reliable and transparent. It definitely increases their efficiency apart from improving the quality of the services provided by our offices. It has been extensively used in govt. offices and some of the successful system that has increased efficiency in our country are;

1. Smart card for driving licenses
2. e-seva in Andra Pradesh where single window facility is available for multiplicity of activities.
3. e-ticket in Railways and Airlines is another outstanding example.
4. e-return of Income Tax department.

Computers and Internet have played a vital role to speed up communication both within and outside the organisation. It should be extensively used and the staff be motivated to learn it and use it. When multiple employees use these modern communication tools the output increase is manifold. It is not only efficient, it is effective also.

Management is efficiency in climbing the ladder of success; leadership determines whether the ladder is leaning against the right wall.
STEPHEN COVEY

Efficiency is doing things right; effectiveness is doing the right things.
PETER DRUCKER

There can be economy only where there is efficiency.
BENJAMIN DISRAELI

"Efficiency tends to deal with Things. Effectiveness tends to deal with People. We manage things, we lead people"

"Obviously, the highest type of efficiency is that which can utilize existing material to the best advantage"
JAWAHARLAL NEHRU

"Earn by your efficiency and enthusiasm, The right to play higher and higher roles, That is the meaning and purpose of life."
SRI SATHYA SAI BABA

91
Capacity Building

Government functions in rapidly developing economy like India needs simultaneous changes at various levels in functions that are supportive or complimentary to the growth process. It involves variety of initiatives which need to be suitably strategised, i.e.

- » Strategy for increasing transparency in all government processes.
- » Goals and objectives of such strategies with necessary procedures developed.
- » Competence building of the bureaucratic machinery.
- » Need to shift from a top down to a more bottom up or horizontal approach.

In the transformational phase and beyond, all bureaucratic organisations need to have a clear approach towards capacity building of its workforce. Such capacity building has the following important functions;

a. It updates the employees on the latest in respective area.
b. The interaction with other colleagues fires up their imagination and breaks the lethargy.
c. It fires them up on a path of constant growth.

This brings in the question of who will do this capacity building, on what aspects, for what duration and at what institution. Experience shows that employees are keen to undergo training in new areas and would like to be trained at the best of places by the best of faculties. Today the states have a large number of public and private sector institutions such as IIT's, IIM's, IIPA, LBSNAA etc apart from scores of discipline specific institutions. Most states have their local state institutes of public administration which can provide training on a diversity of department specific issues. The employees can share their field experiences with the select faculty and clarify their doubts during such trainings.

The exposures to such capacity building courses in itself may bring about a transformation in the individual to seek a totally new path. It would also help him grow as an individual.

Don't limit yourself. Many people limit themselves to what they think they can do. You can go as far as your mind lets you. What you believe, remember, you can achieve.

MARY KAY ASH

Don't quack like a duck. Soar like an eagle.

KEN BLANCHARD

The turning point, I think, was when I really realized that you can do it yourself. That you have to believe in you because sometimes that's the only person that does believe in your success but you.

TIM BLIXSETH

In the new economy, information, education, and motivation are everything.

BILL CLINTON

Follow your own particular dreams. We are handed a life by peers, parents and society, you can do that or follow your own dreams. Life is short, be a dreamer but be a practical person.

HUGH HEFNER

Do not wait; the time will never be "just right." Start where you stand, and work with whatever tools you may have at your command, and better tools will be found as you go along.

NAPOLEON HILL

92

Keep the Team Motivated

Motivation can be defined as the skill of energising yourself and others to accomplish something positive. To be a leader you need to be a motivator of your people and also yourself. As a leader you need to make other people feel better by making him more motivated. You also need to ensure that he continues this link with other persons who come in his contact. Motivation keeps the person energised so that he is on his targets with greater enthusiasm and vigour. Apart from motivating others a leader has to see that he himself is also motivated.

The Process of motivating yourself or someone else involves several stages which lead to a motivated person. First comes developing a vision of success. This vision should be backed by faith & confidence. In such an environment the positive feedback uplifts the confidence and boosts up the motivation process. The motivational path is guided by the vision of success. This vision need to be backed by a brief workable action plan and should not be a something vague. As leader of the team or head of office you need to present this roadmap to success with enthusiasm so that it infuses & energises the team and gives them confidence. Dealing with large workforce in governments it is essential to keep the programmes in good pace or keep the team woven around some common driver. These can be some sort of incentives like money, power, accomplishment, respect, recognition, rewards etc.

The future depends on what we do in the present.
MAHATMA GANDHI

Take heed: you do not find what you do not seek.
ENGLISH PROVERB

Take calculated risks.
That is quite different from being rash.
GEORGE S. PATTON

If you do not hope, you will not find what is beyond your hopes.
ST. CLEMENT OF ALEXANDRA

Seek the lofty by reading, hearing and seeing great work at some moment every day.
THORNTON WILDER

The only way of finding the limits of the possible is by going beyond them into the impossible.
ARTHUR. CLARKE

We are what we repeatedly do. Excellence, therefore, is not an act but a habit.
ARISTOTLE

Work spares us from three evils: boredom, vice, and need.
VOLTAIRE

Experience is the child of thought, and thought is the child of action.
BENJAMIN DISRAELI

Nothing will ever be attempted if all possible objections must first be overcome.
SAMUEL JOHNSON

Nothing great was ever achieved without enthusiasm.
RALPH WALDO EMERSON

93

Competence – Let it Grow All Around

Leadership is not about some vague entity. It is about leading the team of fellow colleagues and subordinates. Leading in government also means that the workforce is professionally trained. Competency in administration not only means focused work; it also means that the persons performing it are focused and clear about what they are dealing with and why a certain course of action is better. Competency among employees has a positive effect on the organisation as a whole, particularly the human resource which is the core of any organisation. For any profession or work place it means whether a person can undertake what is required to be done by him at the desired levels of performance. In a professional scenario it means –

1. That the person has certain desirable technical or professional qualifications which are a precondition for him to be on that job. It usually means the academic qualification.
2. That he has received some professional or work related trainings that make him a more informed or knowledgeable person with respect to others. It may mean having a training in accounting or budget,

financial analysis, project management, or other job specific skill like specialization in handling boiler problems, aircraft air conditioning etc.
3. The person uses those skills in his work place on day to day basis on the issues that are posed to him.

In administrative works it means;

* The person is updated on various laws and regulations that govern his works (such as health manuals, works manuals etc.)
* The person is updated on various guidelines, protocols and instructions issued related to work performance and he uses them at certain desired level of acceptance.

These are used by the competent professional in a routine manner. If one is an engineer, the reference to various manuals indicates that he is aware about the technicalities relating to that work. Similarly a professional approach to a problem would mean studying it from the legal, regulatory and other contexts. It is observed that there is an approach among bureaucracy to deal work in a general manner rather than analysing and arriving on conclusion based on laws, regulations, manuals, guidelines or documented precedence. Professional competence is to been seen in the work done by an individual. His seal of in depth understanding of the issues should speak from the way he deals the problems.

Professional competence is a continuous process which should grow on the individual and should be widely promoted among the employees. It makes the employees approach work in a systematic and methodical way, which have been extensively tested and verified like a professional protocol for an open heart surgery.

Another aspect of professionalism is the competence of interpersonal relationship. All problems or issues have a human aspect too. Ultimately we are dealing with human beings who are working on any issue. These inter personal skills can also be developed and acquired by training programmes. Labour or management issues at time get stuck on issues which require competence of a different nature – The competence of man management. Professional trainings if taken earlier come very handy.

In the bureaucratic type of organisation we regularly come across what is commonly referred as administrative competence which is the above approach applied to administrative tasks. **Administrative or professional competence is an asset that can be grown constantly by each individual. He can constantly update him self by doing new professional or academic courses which can enrich him professionally and academically apart from giving him an edge over other persons.**

"The secret of success is constancy of purpose."
BENJAMIN DISRAELI

"We are what we repeatedly do. Excellence, then, is not an act, but a habit."
ARISTOTLE

"In reading the lives of great men, I found that the first victory they won was over themselves? Self-discipline with all of them came first."
HARRY S. TRUMAN

The future belongs to the competent. It belongs to those who are very, very good at what they do. It does not belong to the well meaning.
BRIAN TRACY

"He conquers twice who conquers himself in victory."
JYRUS

"What lies in our power to do, lies in our power not do."

ARISTOTLE

"The first and the best victory is to conquer self."

PLATO

Unless you change how you are, you will always have what you've got.

JIM ROHN

"You never will be the person you can be if pressure, tension and discipline are taken out of your life."

DR. JAMES G. BILKEY

Administrative or professional competence is an asset that can be grown constantly by each individual. He can constantly update him self by doing new professional or academic courses which can enrich him professionally and academically apart from giving him an edge over other persons.

94

Manage Your Personal Matters

As Principal Secretary to the Government I have to deal with personnel and service matters of thousands of employees. The issues that frequently come up before the government are related to policy but the correspondence in general from employees indicates that a large number of their personal matters remain unresolved. Some typical matters are:-

1. Their Pension case has not been prepared by the department.
2. The balance of provident fund has not been released.
3. Earned leave encashment has not been settled.
4. The accounts relating to advances have not been resolved.
5. Excess Income Tax has been deducted but the refund is not materializing.

These problems relate not only to retired employees the serving employees also have to struggle with similar issues all through their career.

There is no fool proof way to ensure that all your personal matters are resolved but a systematic and well thought approach can help keeping oneself updated. In managing personal matters attention need to be given to the following:-

a. **Maintain Subject wise files** – Files on various matters be made subject wise .These could vary from Leave account, Duplicate service book, Duplicate GPF book, Leave Travel Concession, Home Loan, Car loan, Transfer orders, Charge notes, Property Returns, Correspondence on foreign travel, Income Tax return, Bank related matters, Vehicle Insurance, Personal Insurance, Rent receipts, Water & power bills, Personal academic degrees and study related matters, Annual confidential reports, Licenses etc. This is just an illustration of the type of files a typical government employee needs to maintain.

b. **Periodic review** – These files are of diverse nature and there is no set periodicity about their review. The best course of action is to see this bunch of files every month and see which of them have fallen due. This periodic review also helps in weeding out the useless papers and put in place the new relevant correspondence.

c. **Regular updation** – It is an outcome of the review done periodically. You may find that the Provident Fund/Service book needs a yearly updation, the insurance policy has matured, the car policy is due, the gun licensed needs renewal, the bank fixed deposit receipt has matured, an increment has not been added by the accounts section, the excess tax has not been refunded, the Lease fees is due and Annual property return is to be filed. A list of all such outstanding items can be drawn up and followed up on a daily basis.

d. **Daily monitoring** – So many of the personal and official works add to our daily schedule. These need to be fitted into the day's engagements and completed. Some illustrations can be drawing the money from ATM, Buying train ticket, sending a request for waitlisted ticket, getting a new Identity card prepared, Depositing school fee for your sons etc.

The daily to do list should have your personal works also. You can use your personal staff to get them done while you attend to more demanding affairs of the government. Most offices have Bank, ATM, and Post Office etc. to make life easier. These facilities can be utilized to complete the pending works of the day.

95

Clean Up – Speed Up & Save

I was divisional commissioner at Jabalpur when the 11th Finance Commission allocated about Rs. 45 crores for the development of tourism in the State. One such site was Bhedaghat Waterfall where various development activities were to be undertaken. The funds & various associated delegation were at the local level under the monitoring of the commissioner. We did an elaborate planning exercise supported by necessary awareness through media about its timelines & significance. When the public works department called for the tenders for various works they were amazed to find that the contractors had quoted rates almost 20% less than what was prevailing in that area. We were very happy and when we probed the reason that came out to be was that the promptness of decisions, guidance, monitoring and transparency of the entire process under the guidance of commissioner has given confidence to the contractors that their payment would not be delayed and they can deliver quality work in the stipulated time.

The lesson learnt was that a clear dedicated team not only performs in time, it saves on cost also.

96

Citizen Focused Agenda

All governments are meant to serve the public. It is the citizen centric focus of government that brings laurels to team and their leaders. It is therefore important that leaders in government while drafting the action points should keep its citizens in focus. What are their aspirations and problems that need to be looked into?

Citizen centric nature of governance can find place in all departments and at all levels and would in turn need solutions that are evolved after in depth understanding of the issues with stake holders – The citizens. The citizen focused agenda can be found in almost every department, such as;

1. Revenue-Encroachment on public lands
2. Education-Absenteeism in schools
3. Public health-Seasonal diseases
4. Police-Insensitivity to complaints
5. Irrigation-Water not reaching up to the tail end of canals.
6. Public works-Poor upkeep of public roads and bridges etc.

Departments driven by agenda that give maximum good to the maximum persons are going to be the real heroes in government and it's the responsibility of the leaders to align work priorities with the people agenda.

97

Media – The Friend, Philosopher, Critic and Guide

Media called the fourth estate of democracy has been under criticism from time to time. In the past 2 decades, there had been times when the law to curtail freedom of press was brought before the parliament and rightly dropped at a later date. With the huge growth of electronic technology in the past 20 years the relevance of media has grown manifold. Things get reported and telecasted almost instantaneously. With hundreds of channels competing for viewers it has become the watchful eye of any democracy.

Media has today become an essential component of government. All governments have an elaborate set-up at various levels to ensure that its efforts of good governance are widely reported and appreciated. In practical sense 'Media' is today an integral part of government. They have access to information much quicker and with greater depth than any institution in isolation. Media in totality can therefore be today better described as friend – philosopher, critic and guide.

A friend: Media survives on reliable and substantial information. Leaders in all walk of life are privy to important information. By providing suitable inputs to media they can give timely missing links to important stories which are essential for sustenance of any news agency. Friendship is always two ways. With the inputs which the press has from innumerable sources they are able to identify a small fire and bring it to the notice of those who can douse it, thereby saving millions. The timely reporting of some other story can avert a major catastrophe.

It is always healthy to be friendly to media. They can pick up a good story and provide it a coverage which government on its own can not do. Accessibility is always healthy and beneficial. It keeps the channels of communication always open. When the leadership is accessible and open in communicating with them there is very little scope for mis-reporting and bonafide mistakes, if any also gets corrected promptly by the press. Barring stray exceptions the media men are a positive lot. They have the professional compulsion to look for what is saleable and not what government may like to be written. In all such difficult times accessibility to the press is always better so that reporting gets balanced.

Philosopher – Majority of towns in India have the presence of all major print and electronic media. This network of thousands of media man, photographers and journalists are spread all over the state and their access to information and facts is tremendous. The newspapers and T.V. Channels therefore provide not only what's happening at various places but also critical observation through their columns and editorials. These are extremely educative and thought provoking and can be a very useful tool for all administrators and leaders in departments.

The Critic: Media through its editorials news analysis and other methods provides a platform to diverse spectrum of population to share their views and feelings on everything happening around them. The press being neutral can generally present a balanced picture of the issue. Those in government thus have a better picture of the issue under debate. It helps government in taking timely corrective steps.

Providing a forum to exchange ideas – the press today is global. With the available technology one can share the online information through videos and photos. The developments stories in one part of the globe can be picked up by friends on the other end and use it free of cost. Such idea sharing and picking up new links from other parts is a very useful role played by the media.

Creative and positive proactive interaction should be a constant way of staying in touch with the press. One can do so by taking them on a visit to some work/project site and let them have an on the spot evaluation of what the department has done. Both the partners would be doing their respective jobs and it creates a win-win situation. Regular meet the press sessions are also very useful. Those can be done when a significant land mark has been achieved or a new project launched.

Taken in totality media is all about government and its citizens. It gives a different picture of the departments from a public eye. It really helps in modifying and redesigning the schemes for the better.

"Whoever controls the media controls the mind."
JIM MORRISON

A good newspaper, I suppose, is a nation talking to itself.
ARTHUR MILLER

In the real world, the right thing never happens in the right place and the right time. It is the job of journalists and historians to make it appear that it has.
MARK TWAIN

I fear three newspapers more than a hundred thousand bayonets.
NAPOLEON

Get your facts first, and then you can distort 'em as much as you please.
MARK TWAIN

When a dog bites a man that is not news, but when a man bites a dog that is news.
CHARLES ANDERSON DANA

"For a politician to complain about the press is like a ship's captain complaining about the sea"
ENOCH POWELL

There are only two forces that can carry light to all the corners of the globe... the sun in the heavens and the Press down here.
MARK TWAIN

"The press is the best instrument for enlightening the mind of man, and improving him as a rational, moral and social being"
THOMAS JEFFERSON

98

Reorganise to Optimise

During my posting as commissioner Bilaspur division in one of the monthly revision of the agriculture department I was surprised to find that the average agricultural production for Paddy was around 15 quintal per hectare where as the maximum possible yield for that type of soil was 105 quintal. This was a phenomenal gap of 90 quintal and productivity wise about 6 times. I studied the causes in depth and found that what the 105 quintal per hectares farmers are achieving others can also achieve. The difference between the achievers and the non achievers lied in the approach of optimization i.e.

- » They were enthusiastic cultivators.
- » They chose Better seed.
- » Better soil preparation.
- » Pre treated seed was used.
- » Timely input of measured fertilizers.
- » Pesticides and insecticides were applied according to the identified pests.
- » Watering was regulated & not flood irrigation.
- » Inter cropping with other short duration compatible crops was adopted.
- » Better sowing practices were adopted.

» Use of modern agricultural implements.
» They had the desire to learn new and modern agricultural practices.

On the contrary the farmers with low production were not systematic about seed selection, seed treatment, soil preparation, dosage of fertilizers and irrigation practices. In fact there were instances where excess dose of a particular chemical fertilizer or a pesticide had resulted in serious crop damage.

Looking to the economic conditions of the small & medium farmers and the limited budget available with the department an innovative Zero Cost Packages was evolved. This focused on;

» Imparting constant training to farmers at every stage of the crop
» Educating them about the crop choice & the associated practices based on their available resources.
» It was a zero cost addition proposal supplemented by necessary training doses by officials of agriculture, horticultures & irrigation departments.
» It was an exercise in optimizing the use of seeds, water, fertilizers, pesticide, agricultural implements and the most important the human resource of the farmer.
» It was reducing dosage where it was in excess and increasing where it was inadequate.
» Constant monitoring by the team leader at every stage to ensure timely availability of various inputs.

The results were amazing:–

» There were lesser pest/insects attacks.
» They got additional crop due to intercropping of suitable crops.

» Overall increase in production for every farmer who adopted these practices.
» Lesser consumption of insecticides and pesticides.

It was a tremendous moral booster for all. A zero cost project had yielded millions. All this was achieved by just harmonising and optimizing the available resources.

What was achieved in Bilaspur holds true for all real life situations in government and a close scrutiny of any project can reveal where we need to intervene to modify the inputs. Obviously the result would be far better where additional financial resources can be put in; nevertheless there would be substantial growth across board. The lessons learnt in the above experiments were:

a. Every citizen is interested in improvement.
b. Since the activities are in public domain some officials would have to provide leadership at every level.
c. Close analysis of what goes in and what comes out at what cost is very important to identify weak linkages.
d. Re marshalling and redesigning the inputs without additional cost in itself can lead to significant growth.
e. Constant training and motivation at every level, both to the citizen and to the officials, is essential.
f. The gains are phenomenal and for a project like a 100 days crop the results can be seen in a short span of 100 days.

Optimization is an activity that needs to be done by all officers at all levels. In government we all waste our resources in

- Doing work without much planning
- Letting the office work guide you rather than you guiding the office.
- Not sorting out the bottle necks.

Optimization has been defined as to make the most of or develop to the utmost extent, or obtain the most efficient use of. It can also be described as

> "finding an alternative with the most cost effective or highest achievable performances under the given constraints by maximizing desired factors and minimizing undesired ones."

Optimisation is all the more significant where there is constraint of financial resources. This is commonly the situation in government project. Nevertheless by resorting to the optimization exercise the desired maximisation can be achieved.

99

Show What You Talk – The Photographer Friend

A photograph is more than a photograph. It is freezing the moment in respect of time and space. It shows what you want to show and also what you don't want to show. A photograph is used as it is, nothing more and nothing less.

Camera is a very potent tool for any media man. In fact it is mightier than the gun. The press uses it extensively to show the failures of government on various counts, Health, Education, Law and order, welfare, Security, Development etc. Good news becomes better if it is supplemented by a photograph. Similarly a good report gets more weight if it is supplemented by a nice photograph.

Camera as an inspection tool is very rarely used. Every day we come across various reports on various aspects. It could be the poor quality of construction of a road or a bridge or a school or the state of affairs of a government hospital or the condition of floods in a city, very rarely we find photographs attached with the report to explain what is being said. A photographs is like "Seeing the talking".

Government officials should make regular use of photograph for the following reasons:

1. It captures most of the details about the place and the event.
2. It indicates the general scenario of the location.
3. It also shows unconnected things which can become relevant at a later stage.
4. It is not opinion. It is what is seen.
5. One can take many pictures to indicate different aspects of the same situation.
6. A photograph is a very useful tool to compare a situation over a period of time. It can therefore help in monitoring the physical progress.
7. A photograph is person neutral.

With the rapid growth of mobile phone with multiple features, including camera taking color photographs, photography has become a child's play. Every good mobile not only has a built in camera it has adequate memory also to take enough pictures. So there is no limitation to the 36 or 72 exposure space constraint felt with the film type cameras. It also does away with the burden of carrying an extra person as your camera man apart from the obvious advantage that you select yourself what need to be photographed.

A digital camera is an essential accessory for every government official and it should be used as frequently as possible. With the compatibility of computers all the photographs can be quickly down loaded for future references.

A photograph can also remind you that some good work needs to be appreciated by a letter. Written reports have the limitation that –

1. You have to spend an hour or two to describe all that you saw. The reports can be brief and let the photo do the talking.

2. It takes time to read the details but a photo can explain it in a minute and much more.
3. A photo has a tendency to stay back in the memory.

The digital photographs also have the advantage that they can be quickly transmitted over long distances as an email attachment. This portability of photographs is a very significant tool that can add weight to our reports. The digital cameras have the advantage that one can take as many photographs as one wants and delete those that are not of good quality. A photograph is a speaking document. The face expressions can speak a lot about the environment & the mood of the place.

The Camera can not lie.

HAROLD EVANS.

The camera is an instrument of detection; we photograph not only what we know, but also what we don't know.

LISETTE MODEL

A true photograph need not be explained, nor can it be contained in words.

ANSEL ADAMS

When words become unclear I shall focus with photograph.

ANSEL ADAMS

A good photograph is one that communicates a fact, touches the heart and leaves the viewer a changed person for having seen it. It is, in a word, effect.

IRVING PENN

Camera as an inspection tool is very rarely used. Every day we come across various reports on various aspects. It could be the poor quality of construction of a road or a bridge or a school or the state of affairs of a government hospital or the condition of floods in a city, very rarely we find photographs attached with the report to explain what is being said. A photographs is like "Seeing the talking".

100

The Well Prepared Leader

Preparation always pays. Whether it is the college examination or a routine meeting, the well prepared always has the upper hand. Leaders in government and heads of offices have multifarious responsibilities and in that context it is significant that what is done is done with full preparation. Though preparation helps in all works of life some key meeting, an important interview, a briefing on crucial matter should always be done with an adequate preparation. It means that you have:

1. The back up data on a related issue.
2. One is conversant with the rules and regulation on the subject.
3. You are familiar with the risks involved.

A well prepared can meet the challenges with much confidence and determination than an unprepared. He can also bounce back with greater enthusiasm.

> *What we do on some great occasion will probably depend on what we already are; and what we are will be the result of previous years of self-discipline.*
>
> HENRY PARRY LIDDON

"Prepare for the worst. Plan for the best."
LORRIN L. LEE

"There are no secrets to success. It is the result of preparation, hard work, and learning from failure."
COLIN POWELL

"I'm just preparing my impromptu remarks."
WINSTON CHURCHILL

"If you're not practicing, somebody else is, somewhere, and he'll be ready to take your job."
BROOKS ROBINSON

Spectacular achievements are always preceded by spectacular preparation.
ROGER STAUBACH

I will study and prepare and one day my chance will come.
ABRAHAM LINCOLN

Give me six hours to chop down a tree, and I will spend the first four hours sharpening the axe.
ABRAHAM LINCOLN

How you run the race – your planning, preparation, practice, and performance – counts for everything. Winning or losing is a by-product, and after effect, of that effort.
JOHN WOODEN

To be prepared is half the victory.
MIGUEL DE CERVANTES

The best preparation for tomorrow is doing your best today.
H. JACKSON BROWN JR.

The time to repair the roof is when the sun is shining.
JOHN F. KENNEDY

Madan Mohan Upadhyay, I.A.S. did his Masters in Chemistry from the St. Stephen's College, Delhi University and belongs to the 1981 batch of the Indian Administrative Service. He super annuated from the post equivalent to the Chief Secretary of the state.

He has rich experience of working with the government at important positions like Principal Advisor Institute of good governance, Additional Chief Secretary, Divisional Commissioner, Managing Director and Collector of several districts among significant assignments.

Mr Upadhyay was nominated for the Padma Shri in the year 2004. He is recipient of the Krishi Karman Award, the highest award in the country in agriculture production, from the President of India for leading the state in agriculture production for two consecutive years. He won the Commonwealth Award for Public Administration and Management (CAPAM) in 2008 in Barbados for innovations in public services . He is also an alumnus of the Harvard University.

Mr Upadhyay can be contacted on on email at mmupadhyay60@yahoo.com.

www.ingramcontent.com/pod-product-compliance
Lightning Source LLC
Chambersburg PA
CBHW020629220526
45464CB00001B/78